Growing Closer
density
and sprawl
in the
Boise Valley

Fewer households with children have spiked the demand for small homes on smaller lots and more renters in Boise's downtown. Pictured: alley off Idaho Street and 9th.

growing
closer density and sprawl in the Boise Valley

Todd Shallat
Brandi Burns
Larry Burke, editors

Investigate Boise Student Research Series
Boise State University
College of Social Sciences and Public Affairs

2011

BOISE STATE UNIVERSITY

Todd Shallat, Ph.D.
Investigate Boise series editor
Center for Idaho History and Politics
tshalla@boisestate.edu

Larry Burke
managing editor

Brandi Burns
student editor

Adele Thomsen
art director

David Eberle, Ph.D.
consulting editor

Melissa Lavitt, Ph.D.
Dean, College of Social Sciences and Public Affairs

Boise State University
College of Social Sciences and Public Affairs
1910 University Drive - MS 1925
Boise, Idaho 83725

© 2011

To order copies contact the
College of Social Sciences and Public Affairs
sspadean@boisestate.edu

(208) 426-3776

Cover illutration based on a photo by Ryan Ludwig

The Investigate Boise Student Research Series

The Boise State University College of Social Sciences and Public Affairs proudly sponsors a nine-credit field school for the study of the Treasure Valley. Each summer, about 40 students interact with professors, practitioners and public officials in a storefront classroom downtown. Students tour, investigate and compose documented research papers concerning political and social problems that vex municipal government. Top papers are peer-reviewed and edited for publication. Topics include housing and homelessness, neighborhood preservation, the political economy of energy and natural resources, and the challenge of urban renewal downtown. For information and sponsorship opportunities, contact Dean Melissa Lavitt at sspadean@boisestate.edu; (208) 426-3776.

geniepatra

Roads converge in the cross-disciplinary study of traffic, air quality, rural preservation and the devastation of suburbia's sprawl.

Contents

Introduction
•••••••••••••••••••••

S prawl meant easy living to postwar dreamers of suburban dreams in cul-de-sac subdivisons. It meant patios and lawns. It meant bad air and asthma. It meant towns segregated by income. It meant longer commutes and higher property taxes. Sprawl, to the historian Lewis Mumford, meant conformity and isolation. Sprawl, to the urbanist James Howard Kunstler, meant "the degrading of the public realm."

Sprawl, whatever it was, caught Idahoans off guard. A 2001 *USA Today* ranking of America's most sprawling mid-sized cities placed Boise at No. 3. In 2004, in a Smart Growth "sprawl index" ranking of the Pacific Northwest, the Boise-Nampa-Meridian Metropolitan Statistical Area (MSA) ranked No. 1. Less than one in ten Boiseans lived in neighborhoods dense enough for regular bus service. Only one neighborhood in Meridian and none in Eagle had more than 12 people per acre. In Ada and Canyon Counties, where the average per acre was five, the recent housing boom had aggressively paved the valley's most arable farmland. Statewide, annually, the boom had consumed an expanse of land more than twice the size of Manhattan, enough farmland to grow 885 million pounds of potatoes or 52 million bushels of corn.

Stewards of the Boise Valley laid the blame at the foot of their cars. By 2007, in McMansions and Hubble Homes near big-box shopping centers, the average Boise household took 11 car trips each day. The Seattle-based Sightlines Institute published a study of the Boise Valley that linked car com-

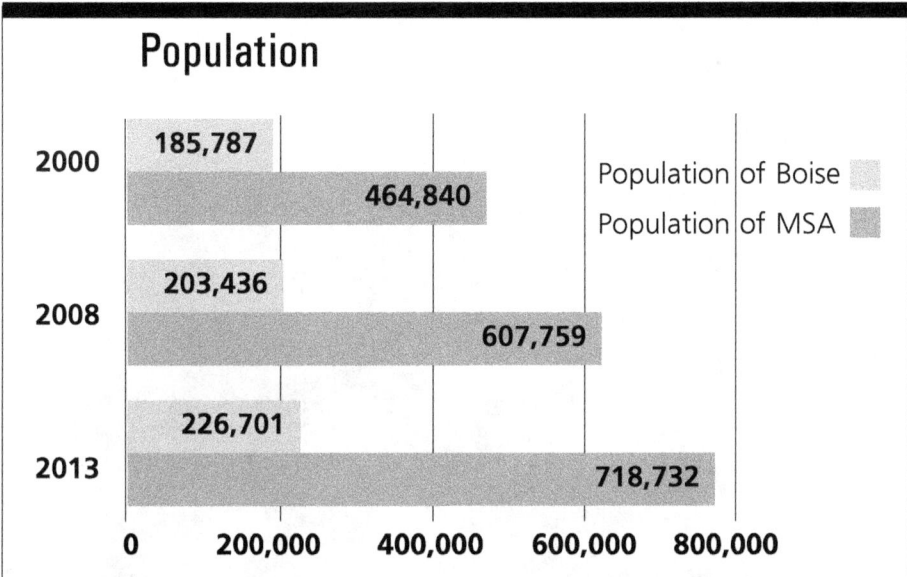

Population

	Population of Boise	
	Population of MSA	

2000 — 185,787 / 464,840

2008 — 203,436 / 607,759

2013 — 226,701 / 718,732

0   200,000   400,000   600,000   800,000

Ada County

Five counties in Southwest Idaho comprise the Boise-Merdian-Nampa Metropolitian Statistical Area (MSA). Commonly called the Treasure Valley, the MSA stretches west from the Boise Foothills to the Oregon boundary line. The Boise Valley more narrowly refers to Ada and Canyon counties.

muting to obesity and diabetes. Air quality also suffered. Yellow ozone alerts in the dangerous summer of 2008 sent Boiseans coughing and wheezing. Toxic dust and soot called "particulate matter" was severe enough for the feds to threaten the county with "nonattainment," black-mark designation that discouraged industrial growth. The City of Boise responded by calling for the power to tax for public transportation. The City of Nampa debated the merits of cutting employees back to four-day workweeks. Caldwell asked winter drivers to scrape icy windshields rather than wait for idling cars to melt off the ice.

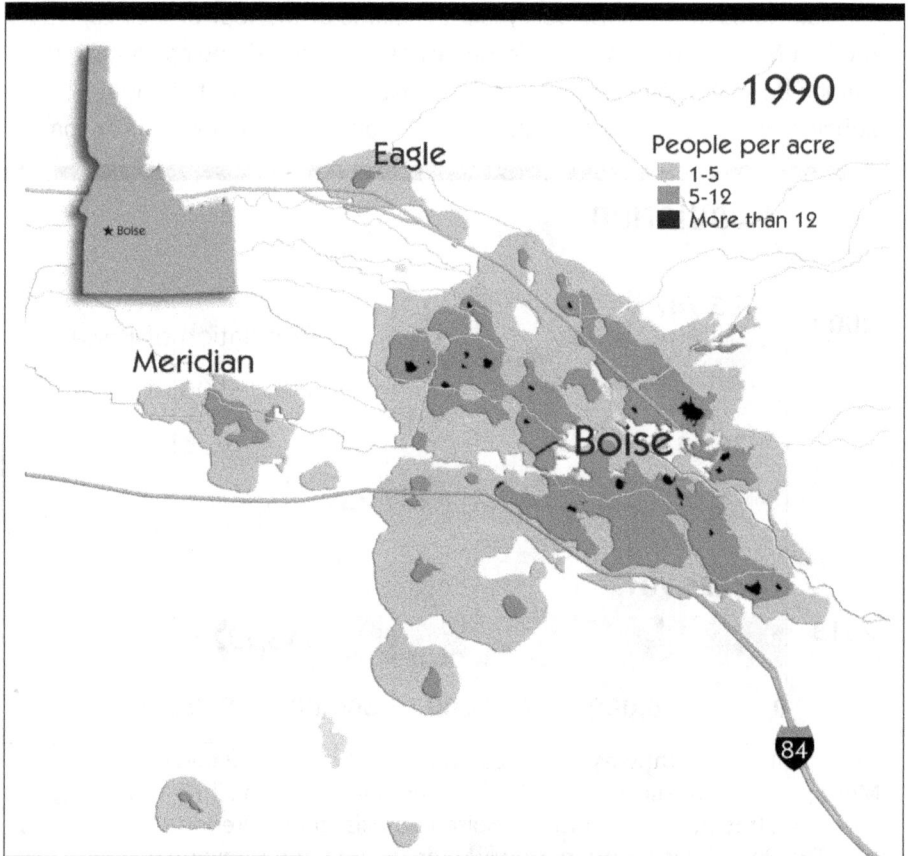

1990

People per acre
- 1-5
- 5-12
- More than 12

Eagle

Meridian

Boise

Boise

★ Boise

84

Sightlines Institute, 2004

From 1990 to 2000, Ada County broke the Northwest record for low-density, car-dependent, energy-consumptive urban sprawl. By 2000 only 7 percent of county residents lived in so-called "compact" transit-friendly neighborhoods with 12 or more people per acre.

In the summer of 2010, in a classroom on Boise's Main Street, sprawl inspired a two-part class on settlement patterns. Forty-four college students from six academic departments wrote documented research papers. Star students returned in the fall to revise and expand their research. *Growing Closer*, herein, presents ten of those student essays. Two trace origins of sprawl. Others consider the politics of infill housing projects and suburbs spread thinly across Ada County by leapfrog development. A photo essay

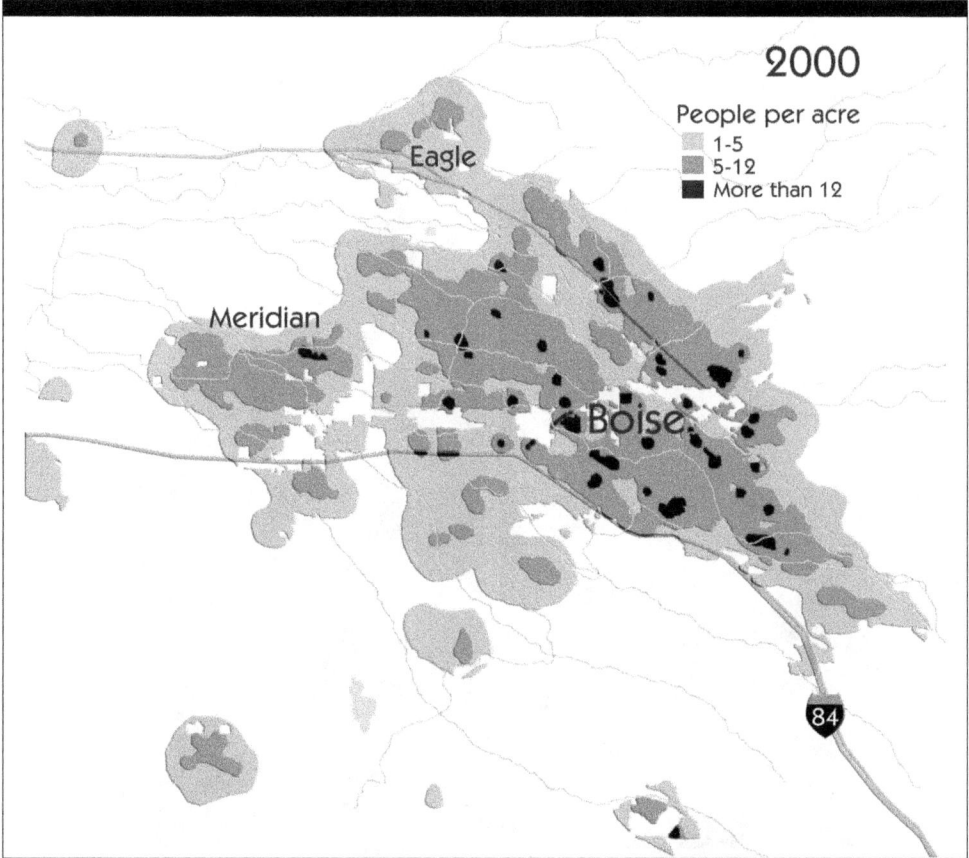

2000

People per acre
1-5
5-12
More than 12

Eagle

Meridian

Boise

84

Sightlines Institute, 2004

recalls sprawl's effect on Emmett's farms. Published by the Boise State University College of Social Sciences and Public Affairs, the book is Volume Two in a student series about people and places transformed by metropolitan growth.

Todd Shallat, Ph.D., directs the Center for Idaho History and Politics at Boise State University. His Boise writings include *Ethnic Landmarks: Ten Historic Places that Define the City of Trees* (2007).

David Eberle, Ph.D., directs the Environmental Finance Center at Boise State University. An economist, he serves on Boise City Council and the board of directors for the Capital City Development Corporation.

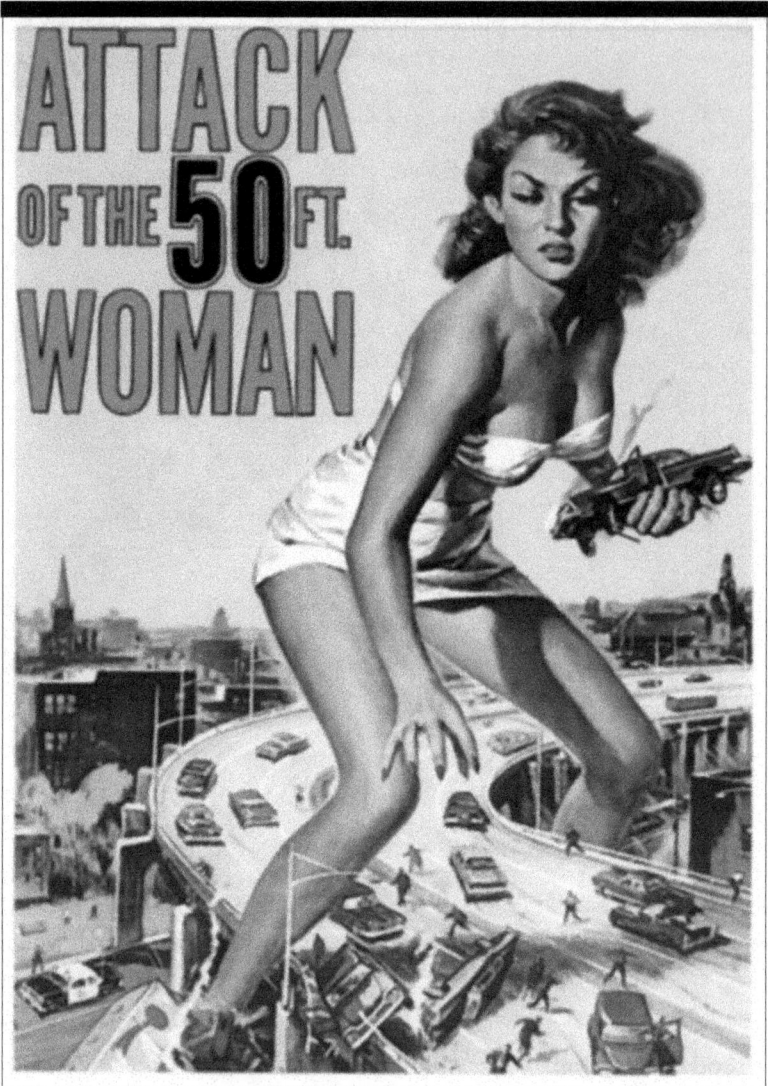

Reynold Brown

A giant alien housewife tramples suburban Los Angeles in *The Attack of the 50-foot Woman*, 1958.

Suburbia's
SPRAWL
by Brandi Burns

growing Closer: Density and Sprawl in the Treasure Valley asks the essential question that faces every city in the midst of sprawling growth: what is the appropriate capacity of the land? The location of the land itself provides an answer. Appropriate capacity depends on where the land is—rural areas have a very low density whereas urban areas have a higher density. Defining the capacity of the land is essential to managing sprawl and enhancing the sustainability of cities.

The growth pattern termed "urban sprawl" in the language of city planning is most commonly an auto-dependent suburb with low-density single-family housing, a bedroom community where few people work. Sprawl often jumps away from the edges of cities. Planners refer to a pattern of housing that "leapfrogs" over open land. Critics denounce that pattern as the antithesis of responsible growth. Sprawl, the critics maintain, has paved over valuable farmland. It puts a strain on infrastructure and fosters an unsustainable dependency on oil and the car. Yet sprawl is deeply ingrained

Radburn, New Jersey, was among the first suburbs designed for the automobile. Platted in 1928, it pioneered cul-de-sacs.

in suburban culture. Encouraged by the dream of homeowners, the love of cars and the longing for freedom of movement, it grows from deeply American roots.

The phenomenon predates the advent of the automobile. Historians trace modern sprawl to wealthy garden suburbs on the outskirts of industrial towns. Historian Sam Bass Warner, Jr., in a famous book about the advent of streetcars, showed how Boston became suburban through a network of electric rails. Boiseans followed Boston's example with streetcars looping west through orchards and farm communities. Ustick, Collister, Star, Geckeler, South Boise, Nampa, Meridian, Middleton and Caldwell were once tied to the capital city through electric streetcar lines.

By 1900, in Boise, Boston and elsewhere, promoters heralded streetcar suburbanization as a modern way to develop the land. Streetcar suburbs, said promoters, combined the open air of the spacious countryside with electricity, paved streets, sewers and other amenities of the city. Richard Hurd, author of *Principles of City Land Values* in 1903, described how residential developments were built on the fringes of cities, which encouraged the more influential social classes to relocate there. Cities took on a star shape as residential houses clustered together around major transportation routes, often traveled by streetcars. These routes frequently became the same ones that cars now use. Historian Jon Peterson has described the turn-of-the-century cities as "great, center-dominated realms in which most commercial and retail activity concentrated at the core, as if drawn by a magnet, and residential functions dominated the periphery, as if expelled by the same force field." Then as now, the centrifugal force of downtown commerce meant cheaper land prices on the periphery.

The New Jersey suburb of Radburn was one of the first built for the car. Opened in 1928, it pioneered superblocks, cul-de-sac streets and block-interior parks. Although the Great Crash of 1929 stunted suburbanization, the planned community movement

American Society of Landscape Architects

The 1929 plan for the proto-suburb of Radburn showed the segregation of housing from industry and stores.

survived. After 1933, with federal subsidies for housing and urban projects, New Dealers planned "garden cities" or "greentowns" surrounded by open land. City and farm would merge in these landscaped suburbs. Radburn would be the model for other towns intended to address the needs of the rural and urban poor. New Dealers planned 19 utopian greentowns. Only three—Greenbelt, Maryland; Greenhills, Ohio; and Greendale, Wisconsin— were actually built.

Greendale, Wisconsin, came to epitomize that New Deal suburban ideal. A Vivian Husher poem paid tribute to suburbs:

Associated Press

Federal highway and housing subsidies sprawled suburbs across Long Island's municipal boundary lines. In 1947, a gallon of gas was 23 cents, a Ford coupe sedan was $1,300 and Levittown's phase one of 2,000 houses sold out in two days.

Should you ask why we love Greendale,
Find it fun to work and play here,
We all answer, we all tell you...
It's awakening to bird-song
In the rosy dawn of springtime!
Watching frisky squirrels cavorting!
Romping space for pets and children,
Far from city's threatening traffic!
It's group picnics at grounds southward,
And the suppers cooked o'er charcoal
In one corner of our gardens;
Baby's playpen in the sunshine,
Knowing well that naught can harm him!

Associated Press

Bill Levitt's suburb came to epitomize white-flight from the inner city and post-war consumerism. Covenants still excluded people of color long after the U.S. Supreme Court struck down segregation in 1954.

New Dealers saw a science in suburban planning. In 1939, in his book *The Structure and Growth of Residential Neighborhoods in American Cities*, Homer Hoyt set out to explore city development, particularly as it concerned the development of neighborhoods. His main issue was whether or not "there is segregation of different types of dwelling units in definite areas, or whether the American urban community contains a hodgepodge of all kinds of residences in all parts of the city." He became concerned with the way cities develop because he found that the richer classes moved to the periphery of the city, leaving behind buildings to be occupied by the poorer classes, in turn depreciating the value of those buildings.

The postwar housing boom and a sharp increase in car ownership extended suburbia's sprawl. Suburbs began to surface in popular culture. The movie *It's a Wonderful Life*, released in 1946, chronicled the worldly dreams of small-town banker George Bailey, who eventually built an afford-

Architect Andrés Duany promoted Seaside, Florida, as the "neo-traditional" antidote to low-density sprawl. Walkable and compact, Seaside inspired a Hollywood spoof called *The Truman Show*.

able-housing suburb called Bailey Park to provide an alternative to Potter's slums, and in turn made the American dream of home ownership possible for many. But praise for the suburban ideal was hardly universal. One critical account came from Hal Burton of *The Saturday Evening Post*. Burton, writing in 1955, scorned the "utter confusion to be found wherever people have moved to the suburbs, which [were] virtually everywhere. Suburban growth was "zestful but disorderly." Burton feared suburbs might fail because of their dependence on cars, because the houses all looked the same, because of inadequate sewers and the over-reliance on septic tanks. Yet he closed on a hopeful note: "There are troubles aplenty, but time and money will solve them all, if ever the boom slows down. When that time comes, suburbia may finally be able to live up to its reputation. Meanwhile, people will grumble about the suburbs, and people will continue to stay there."

Authors Jane Jacobs and Lewis Mumford were among the first to directly link suburban sameness to housing sprawl. In 1961, Jacobs denounced the dangers of sprawl in *The Death and Life of Great American Cities*, an indictment of highways and urban renewal. Jacobs claimed that

America went awry by "replacing, in effect, each horse on the crowded city streets with half a dozen or so mechanized vehicles, instead of using each mechanized vehicle to replace half a dozen or so horses." The result was a "slothful" overabundance of cars. Speedy but inefficient, the vehicles were "choked by their own redundancy." Horses in the crowded city moved almost as fast as cars.

Another critique of technological overdependence was Mumford's *The City in History*, also published in 1961. The historian Mumford saw suburbs as the result of mass production of prefabricated housing. Suburbs had become "a multitude of uniform, unidentifiable houses, lined up inflexibly, at uniform distances, on uniform roads, in a treeless communal waste, inhabited by people of the same class, the same income, the same age group, witnessing the same television performances, eating the same tasteless pre-fabricated foods from the same freezers, conforming in every outward and inward respect to a common mold, manufactured in the central metropolis." Postwar Americans suburbs had been "alienated" from the culture of historic cities. Flight to the suburbs continued, nevertheless, as states added lanes to the highways and white families segregated around whiter suburban schools.

The critiques of suburbia's sprawl in the wake of Jacobs and Mumford were increasingly environmentally based. Mumford sounded the first alarm when he warned that suburban growth would "undermine our historic cities and deface the natural landscape." Suburbs would create "a large mass of undifferentiated, low-grade urban tissue, which in order to perform even the minimal functions of the city, will impose a maximum amount of private locomotion, and incidentally, push the countryside ever further away from even the suburban areas." A movement was started to limit sprawl through the preservation of open space. One plea for growth boundaries came from a 1973 Rockefeller Foundation task force report on urban land use. Another critic of sprawl was the architect Peter Blake. In *God's Own Junkyard*, published in 1979, Blake foresaw "the wholesale destruction of our countryside."

Concern for suburbia's sprawl included a fear of "white flight" social stratification. "An unusual set of circumstances in the United States helped to ensure that suburban areas in the second half of the 20th century would be segregated by income, race and lifestyle," wrote historian Peter Jackson in 1985. Jackson's sweeping history of American suburbanization detailed the restrictive zoning and housing laws that kept people of color from sharing white suburbs. Parkways and expressways promoted segregation either by avoiding or bisecting inner cities. Standardized suburban tract housing, meanwhile, had segregated homeowners by income. Unwritten codes and discrimination kept whites and blacks living apart.

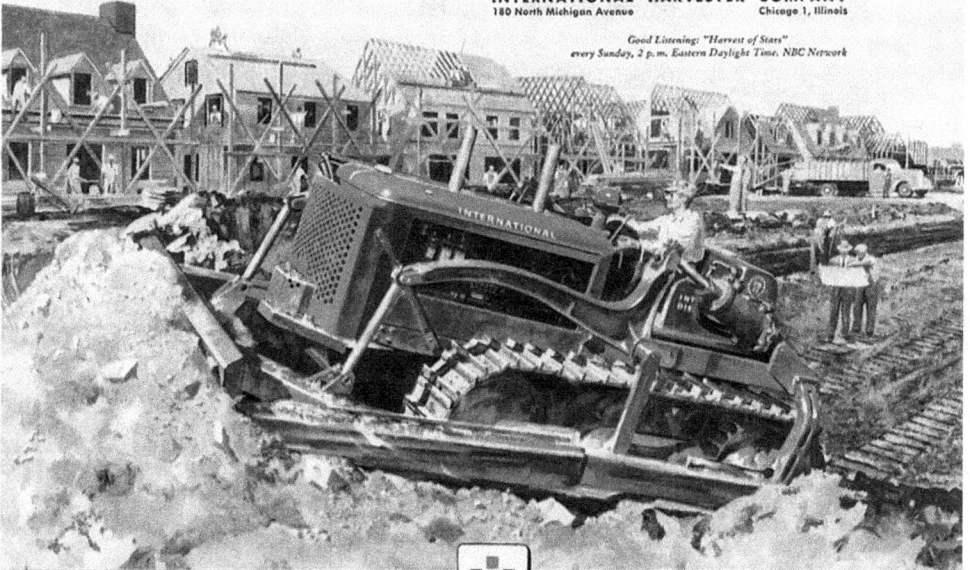

INTERNATIONAL CRAWLERS

Excavate for *Houses by the Block*

AMERICA'S BUILDERS know their business.

They know how to build the best buildings in the world—and quick! They are past masters in the use of modern methods and equipment to speed their work.

When they get the materials and tools they need, their unequaled skill, ingenuity and resourcefulness will quickly provide the housing facilities the American people require.

Typical of practices that speed this modern construction is the use of **International Diesel** Crawler Tractors for excavating. Equipped with bulldozer blades, these powerful tractors take on whole city squares and excavate for houses by the block! They shave off the fertile topsoil and move it aside for later use. They dig out the stubborn subsoil and hardpan. When the foundations of the buildings are set, these master machines backfill with excavated material. Finally, they spread the topsoil back on the surface and landscape the yards for lawns and gardens.

Presto! Houses in the modern manner!

Yes, hats off to the Builders of America ... and to the operators of **International Diesel** Crawlers who prepare the way. It's a winning combination ... an all-American team that will soon have houses built ... houses by the block!

Industrial Power Division
INTERNATIONAL HARVESTER COMPANY
180 North Michigan Avenue   Chicago 1, Illinois

Good Listening: "Harvest of Stars"
every Sunday, 2 p.m. Eastern Daylight Time. NBC Network

Other International Harvester Products... **IH** *Motor Trucks...Refrigeration...Farm Power and Equipment*

INTERNATIONAL *Industrial Power*

Post-war housing transformed the suburban landscape. Pictured: advertisement *Colliers*, 1946.

Architects and planners joined the critique with nostalgic pleas for a return to neighborly streets that predated suburbanization. The critique draws strength from the Congress for the New Urbanism, founded in 1993. Self-styled New Urbanists advocate pedestrian-friendly streets in compact communities. Some emphasize mixed-use developments that combine housing, commerce and schools. Others are chiefly concerned with mass transit. All oppose government policies that pave over rural land and promote inefficient low-density housing.

Critics of sprawl often maintain that government subsidies for highways discourage responsible growth. When residents of a community or a region are spread out over vast distances, it is hard to support a viable bus or rail system. Other transportation options like bicycling or walking become impractical. During the housing boom of the mid-2000s subdivisions grew at unprecedented rates, often at the sacrifice of farmland and small towns that became bedroom communities. But this growth came to a halt as the economy fell into recession three years ago, much like the Great Depression hampered the growth of subdivisions like Radburn, New Jersey. As the building boom slowed with the economy, there were more calls to increase density by infilling empty lots in established cities before developing land on the rim of cities. Density, a measure of how many buildings and people are on a specific amount of land, is just a number and is difficult to visually and spatially imagine. The concept is complicated because many people do not want the density of their neighborhoods increased. But density affects the sustainability of a community. If appropriate density can be achieved, then the community can become "livable" in New Urbanist terms, which means that the residents would be within reasonable walking, biking or public transit distance to quality jobs, affordable housing, shopping and entertainment. Well-designed infill projects that increase density can reduce outward sprawl.

The recent focus on sustainable and livable communities has resulted in steps at the federal level to manage sprawl. The Interagency Partnership for Sustainable Communities was formed in 2009 by the Department of Housing and Urban Development, the Department of Transportation and the Environmental Protection Agency. The federal agencies formed the partnership to "help improve access to affordable housing, more transportation options and lower transportation costs while protecting the environment in communities nationwide," according to its website. The partnership has identified six livability principles to guide its efforts: (1) provide more transportation choices; (2) promote equitable, affordable housing; (3) enhance economic competitiveness; (4) support existing communities; (5) coordinate and leverage federal policies and investment; and (6) value communities and

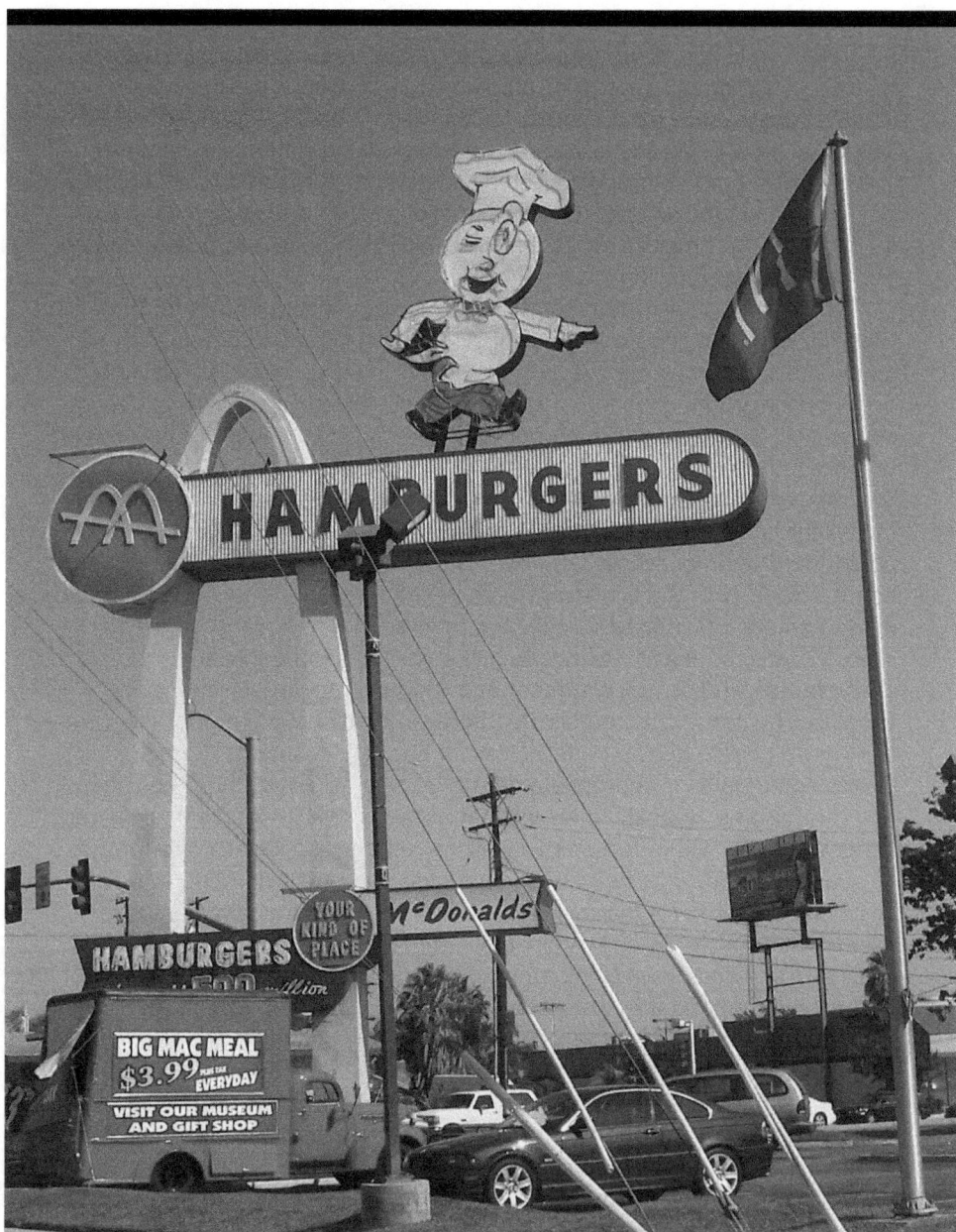

Denise Ramirez

Opened in 1953 in Downey, California, the world's oldest McDonalds still has golden arches and a neon "Speedee" sign. Fast-food drive-ins of the 1950s and '60s shadowed suburbia's sprawl.

neighborhoods. These principles will combine to create more sustainable communities by offering transportation options in combination with affordable housing to decrease commuting costs and by providing quality jobs in communities. The three federal agencies individually can only fight sprawl on a limited level, but the partnership allows a more aggressive and holistic approach, resulting in a higher quality of life for residents choosing higher density places to live.

Some reformers see an expanded role for the U.S. Department of Agriculture. Sprawl becomes an agricultural problem when the loss of farmland destroys the local food economy. If the interagency partnership included the Department of Agriculture, a seventh livability principle could be added, and it would read something like this: promote and support local farmers, especially family farmers, to provide communities with healthy local produce. The Department of Agriculture may not be a part of the current partnership, but some of their programs, especially Know Your Farmer, Know Your Food, may begin to bring local produce closer to residents of nearby communities and provide an economic stimulus.

In the Boise Valley the issue of sprawl pervades most every policy debate over the highest and best use of land. Sprawl aggravates traffic. It clouds the valley with dangerous air. Sprawl also poses problems related to flood control, mass transit, gas prices, infill housing, the food economy and local control. *Growing Closer* offers ten case-study examples of sprawl-related controversy. Each is a story of the local response to auto-dependence and traditional patterns of growth.

• • •

Brandi Burns is the graduate "City Historian" for the Boise City Department of Arts and History. A native of Centerville, she is studying for a master's degree in applied historical research at Boise State University. She earned an honors BA from Idaho State University.

The Boise streetcar brought electricity to West End housing developments. By 1910, three rival streetcar companies rushed to complete the 64-mile loop from Boise to Caldwell.

Streetcar
SUBURBS
by Tully Gerlach

Although relatively young, the boom cities of the American West experienced such swift growth that by the early 20th century they already exhibited patterns of suburban development. Despite being the smallest and most isolated city of the rising urban West, Boise was no exception. Founded in 1863, Boise's location in the southwestern region of the Idaho Territory positioned it as the commercial, financial and political hub of the surrounding mining and agricultural economy. When the city experienced a growth boom from 1890-1910, the surge in population created a demand for homes and land that drove the development of the city's first suburban expansion. The additions on Boise's western end in the early 20th century started a new, progressive suburban form of development that brought the city a new shape and a mature self-concept. The earliest additions to Boise followed a typical 19th century "walking city" development pattern in which mass transit was not yet established and neighborhoods needed to remain close enough to the downtown core for

citizens to commute to work by foot. The establishment of a streetcar sys-
tem in 1891 allowed for residential development further out from the center.
The first suburban additions of the 1890s appeared to the north and east of
downtown, following the early streetcar lines that served Warm Springs
Avenue to the east, the address of choice for the city's wealthy, and 13th
Street to the north, serving properties owned by Franklin Pierce, the city's
largest developer. Despite the open space around the new North and East
End additions, they maintained the standard 25-foot-wide lot pattern of the
original townsite, itself a copy of the standard eastern city lot allocation
method. This older pattern allowed for a great deal of flexibility and density
in rapidly growing American cities, giving owners and speculators more units
of sale per block and offering the chance to maximize profits. Small lots benefitted individual land buyers too, for they could purchase as many lots as
they needed for the business or home they intended to build.

Just after the turn of the century, Boise's West End—the area south of
State Street and north of Fairview Avenue that includes 19th through 32nd
streets—began to take shape. The additions of the new century took on a
new, more recognizably suburban appearance, with lots platted at 50-foot
widths. Comparable in price to the 25-foot lots to the north and east, these
larger lots opened a new opportunity for a broad range of classes to enjoy a
suburban lifestyle. The creation and expansion of streetcar lines increased
this opportunity as they enabled growth in the West End. From its 1891 ori-
gin into the early decades of the 20th century, the streetcar service freed
workers and laborers from the necessity of living within walking distance of
their jobs. Affordable and efficient transit drove growth and made suburban
living accessible and convenient for nearly all classes of citizens.

Development in the West End began with the platting of the Fairview
Addition in 1903, and to its immediate west, the West Side Addition in
1905. Both additions sat in a broad portion of the Boise River floodplain
called the Broadway Terrace, which extended from the current Ann Morrison
Park to Glenwood Street. Originally the site of the local fairgrounds in the
late 19th century, the West End portion of the Broadway Terrace sloped
gradually away from the western edge of downtown toward the Boise River,
a unique geography that made for a prime suburban location. Unlike the
North and East Ends, whose proximity to the Foothills made for marshy,
uneven land prone to flash floods, the West End sat in a large expanse of
flat plain. Despite their location within the Broadway Terrace floodplain,
Fairview and West Side were not at risk for regular flooding, and the vast
gravel deposits left behind by the geological processes that carved out the
terraces of the Boise River made for particularly fertile soil. Just to the north

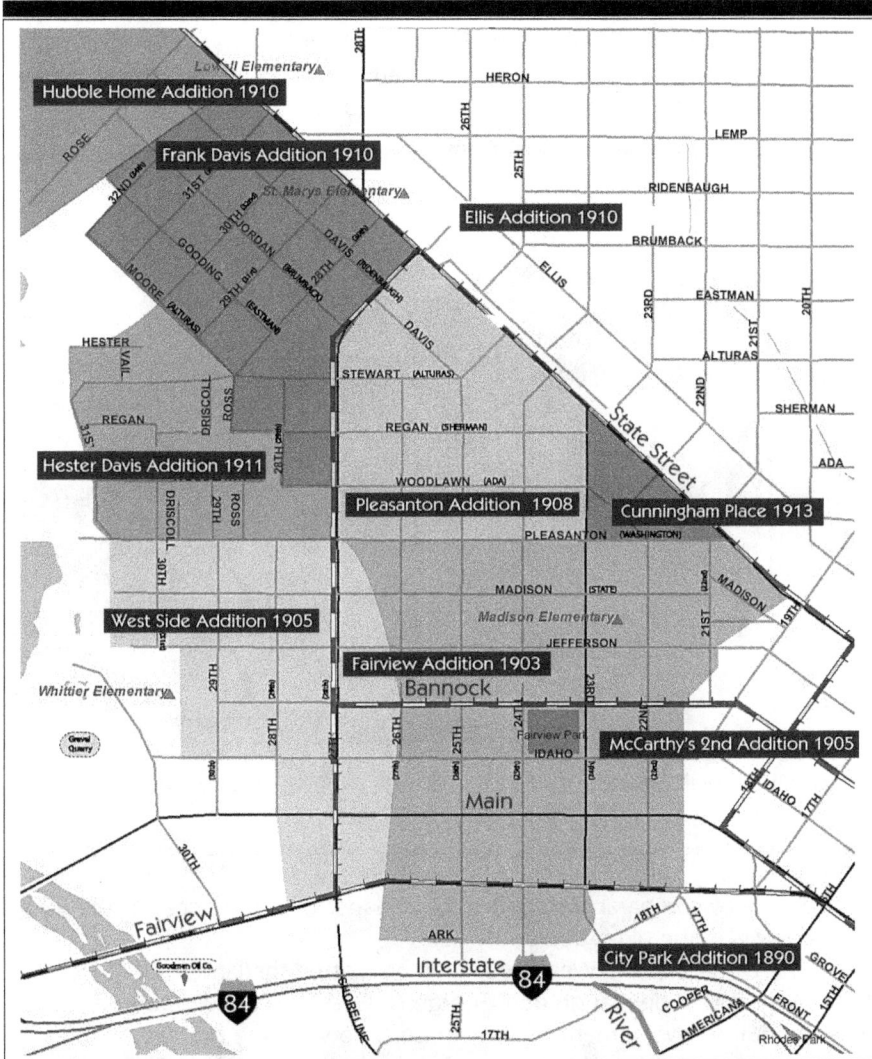

Tully Gerlach

Hubble Home Addition 1910
Frank Davis Addition 1910
Ellis Addition 1910
Hester Davis Addition 1911
Pleasanton Addition 1908
Cunningham Place 1913
West Side Addition 1905
Fairview Addition 1903
McCarthy's 2nd Addition 1905
City Park Addition 1890

Lowell Elementary
St. Mary's Elementary
Madison Elementary
Whittier Elementary

HERON
LEMP
RIDENBAUGH
BRUMBACK
EASTMAN
ALTURAS
SHERMAN
ADA
State Street
DAVIS
STEWART (ALTURAS)
REGAN (SHERMAN)
WOODLAWN (ADA)
PLEASANTON (WASHINGTON)
MADISON (STATE)
JEFFERSON
Bannock
Fairview Park
IDAHO
Main
ARK
Fairview
Interstate 84
River
Rhodes Park
HESTER
VAIL
REGAN
DRISCOLL
ROSS
GOODING
JORDAN
MOORE (ALTURAS)

Boise's streetcar suburbs jumped west of downtown and south of
Valley Road (now State Street) with the Fairview Addition of 1903.

of each addition, early settlers Frank and Hester Davis kept a large farm on
which they grew fruit, cultivated hay and raised sheep. With the Davis
acreages offering a pastoral foreground to the foothills further north and the

city center still close enough to be convenient by means of the streetcar, the first developers of the West End could market their land as the perfect sub-urban combination of rural peace and urban access, available to all. Fairview Addition lots, platted at 50 x 122 feet, went for a standard price of $150

Idaho State Historical Society

Four-room Lowell Elementary School with its dirt playground opened on North 28th Street in 1913.

per lot, a price comparable to and often cheaper than the prices of the 25 x 115 feet lots in the older additions.

The owners of the West Side Addition platted the land for a mix of uses. William H. Ridenbaugh and George H. Gess, successful entrepreneurs involved in the development of early Boise, co-owned the property along with their wives Mary and Catherine. The location of the West Side Addition, with the river at its western edge and the Oregon Short Line spur railway running through its southern portion, made it an ideal site for industrial uses. Freight lines adjacent to or even within industrial property facilitated easy delivery and transport of heavy goods and the river suited industries that required a convenient and reliable waste-removal system. Ridenbaugh and Gess may have originally intended to establish some sort of commercial or industrial interest on the site, Ridenbaugh already owning a successful lumber yard and Gess maintaining a controlling interest in a large-scale meat packing and retail business. The two men, however, could not agree on how to suitably divide the land for commercial development and in light of the city's pressing growth, opted instead to plat most of it for residential use. The Ridenbaughs and Gesses platted their new addition in 50-foot lots and priced them as low as $50 per lot. Within a month of the initial platting, real estate broker D.H. Moseley reported selling at least six lots to "parties of comparatively small means, whose purpose is to build homes in the near future." Along with the large, low-priced lots available in Fairview Addition, West Side opened a new opportunity to people of "small means" to live on large lots in a suburban neighborhood.

Advertisement for Pleasanton Addition, May 1910.

Despite the West End's rural aspect and easily developed land, the presence of the railroad and river undermined its suburban character. The North and East Ends may have been irregular in grade and flood-prone, but they were well removed from major commercial and industrial activity. Having the Boise River on its western border and the main railroad spur line to its south opened the West End to industry at its edges. Just north of the railway ran Fairview Avenue, a major east-west route between Boise and the communities further west and the only river crossing connecting downtown to the western Bench plateau. The proximity of two major transit routes suited commercial development, which filled in the southern stretches of the

Otto Kitsinger

Flat land near the Oregon Short Line made the district well suited for industrial use. Pictured; former concrete factory site at 30th and Pleasanton. Opposite: advertising the Fairview Addition, 1921.

West End from shortly after their initial platting to the present day. Recognizing this potential, the Ridenbaughs and Gesses platted the lots that encompassed the railroad right-of-way in large, irregular shapes suitable for industrial uses. In 1906, the Coast Lumber Company established a finished carpentry mill reputed to be one of the largest in the Pacific Northwest on a large lot south of Fairview and east of the riverbank, where they operated until the 1920s. When Idaho embarked on a concerted program of highway construction beginning in 1914 and continuing on into the 1930s, it designated Fairview as a state and later national highway. In 1926, the Transportation Department established equipment storage and materials test-

ing laboratories on the former site of the Coast Mill. During the same period, at least six oil companies built tank sites in the river bottoms south of Fairview. The Goodman Oil Company—the facilities of which still stand today just east of the Fairview Bridge—placed no fewer than 14 gasoline storage tanks on the riverbank.

At the western edge, the Boise River posed another threat to the West End's suburban character. Even after city annexed the Fairview and West Side Additions around 1912, the riverbanks remained outside the city limits until the 1960s. Their location outside city limits freed riverside industries from what few industrial restrictions existed in Boise in the early 20th century, the chief of which was the ban on slaughterhouses. From Boise's founding until well into the late 20th century, the Boise River, far from being considered the civic and environmental amenity it is today, was viewed as unfit for residential development and best suited as an industrial waste and sewage-removal system. Slaughterhouses, like the later oil tank farms, generated a great amount of effluent and used the river as a dumping ground. By 1912, two slaughterhouses operated on the riverbank at the western edge of the West Side Addition, one an extensive outfit with stock pens and a sausage factory. By the 1930s, the Quinn-Robbins Company purchased the riverside land, closed the slaughterhouses and began excavation of the rich gravel stores of the Broadway Terrace. Until the late 1980s, gravel quarries and a later cement plant, with the attendant noise, pollution and traffic, operated on the West End's western flank. From the beginning, the steady presence of heavy industry effectively stalled residential development in the area. Although by 1912 several modest homes had been built on the West Side's eastern edge, just adjacent to the 27th Street streetcar line and Fairview Addition, the bulk of early West End development happened centrally, in Fairview and the Pleasanton Addition of 1908.

With the development of the Pleasanton Addition, the West End lost its rural aspect, but grew into a new role as a Progressive Era suburb. When streetcar building in Boise began, Hester Davis granted a right-of-way through her rural property in order to connect the Valley Road—State Street today—to Fairview Avenue by means of what became 27th Street. By 1908, with the streetcar lines complete, Davis, 17 years a widow and approaching 70 years of age, finally shut down her farming operations and subdivided her land into the Pleasanton Addition. Though adjacent to the Fairview Addition and maintaining its 50-foot lot pattern, Pleasanton at first aligned closer to the Ellis Addition platted in 1906 in standard 25-foot lots just across Valley Road in the North End. With Boise still in the midst of its 20-year boom of 1890-1910, Pleasanton and Ellis became the additions of choice for Boise's growing middle class and the bungalow was their preferred style of home. Of all residential architectural styles appearing in the city during the 1910s, the popular bungalow exemplified the aesthetics and aspirations of the new middle class of the West. Originally designed to serve as attractive and efficient housing for the working class, the style and versatility of the bungalow, with its open floor plan, built-in cabinets and bookcases, broad porches and balanced structure, appealed to Americans in the prosperous early years of a new century. In October 1909, the *Idaho Statesman* ran a story on the "unprecedented growth" in building of the previous year. "Structures Are Modern And Very Substantial," proclaimed the sub-headline. An entire section covered "Bungalow Construction," noting that these "homes are scattered all over the city from Pleasanton addition on the west to Eden Home and the East Side additions to the east." Many of these bungalows still stand today throughout the Pleasanton and Fairview Additions, contributing to a varied streetscape of intact homes representing some of

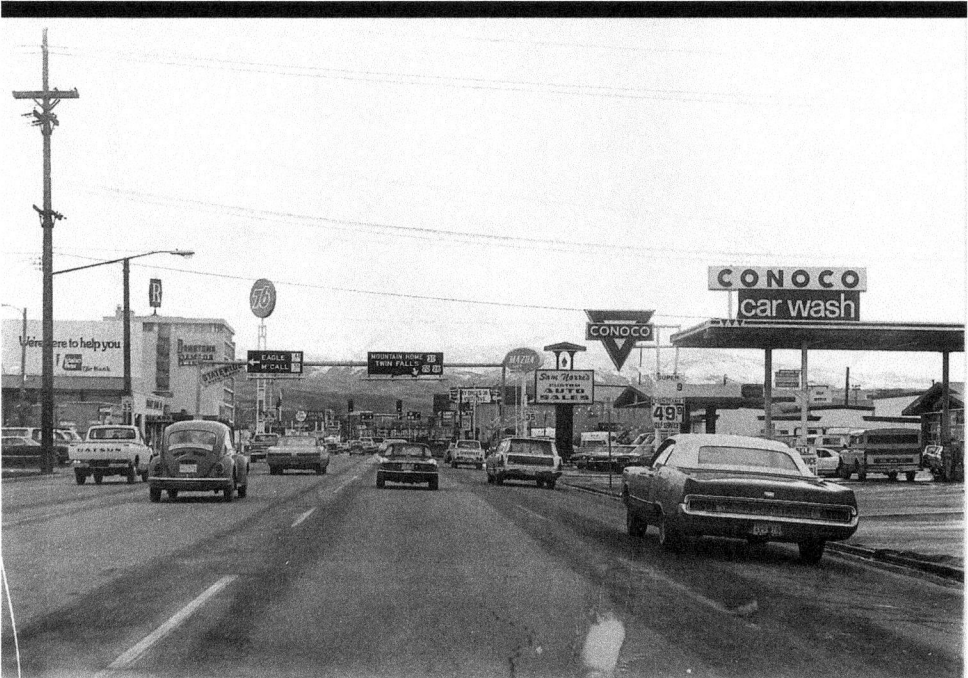

Capital City Development Corporation

The 1928 demise of the streetcar made Fairview an arterial to the new Boise-Nampa highway. Pictured: traffic on Fairview at 23rd, 1975.

the best of early- to mid-20th century residential architecture. As Pleasanton developed, its residents brought a new civic consciousness to bear on the suburban ideal. By 1911, they formed a Pleasanton Club dedicated to the promotion and improvement of their neighborhood. In 1912, the residents of Pleasanton joined with those of Ellis to petition for annexation into the city.

Until the 1960s, Boise's City Charter prohibited the city from forcibly annexing contiguous neighborhoods. Additions wishing to be part of the city were required to petition the city for entry and then to hold a vote among residents. Many additions, such as Fairview and West Side, went through the

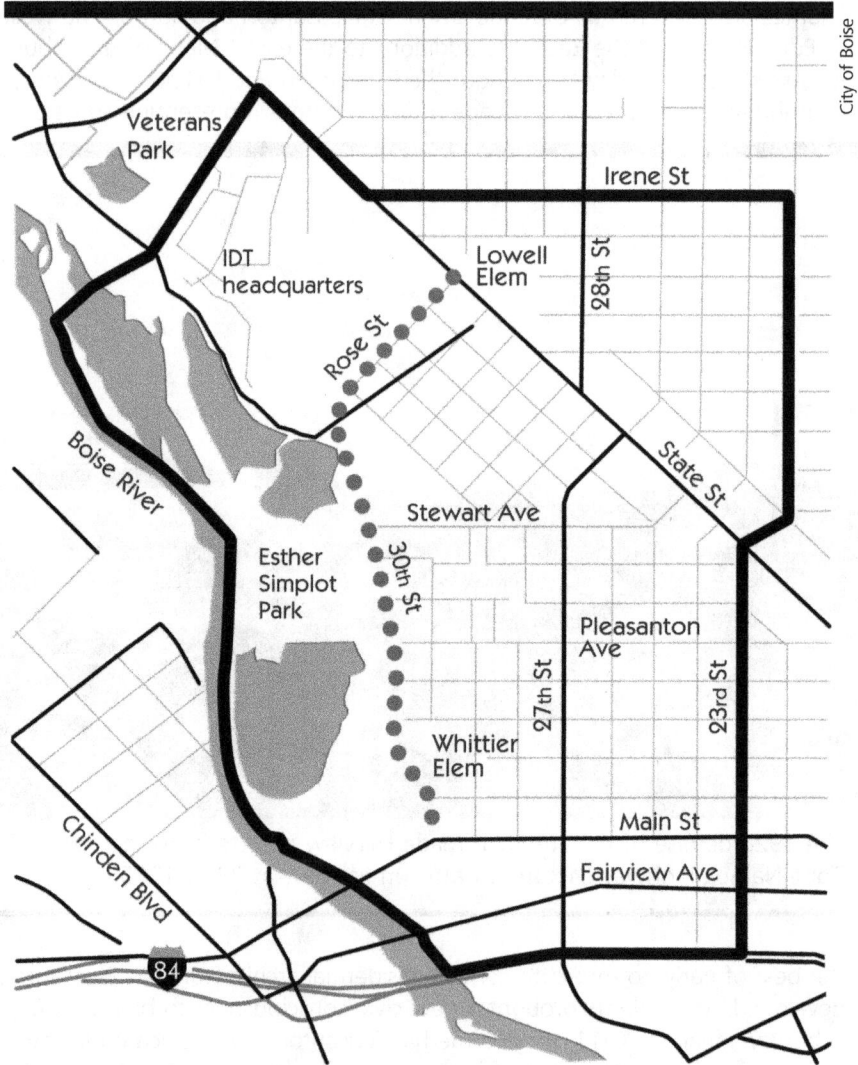

City of Boise

The West End braces for redevelopment road projects, shopping nodes, and a riverside water park. Decades in the making, the plan calls for 30th Street to connect with Fairview and Main.

process with little fanfare, but Pleasanton and Ellis made a public affair of it, with formal presentations to the City Council, vigorous lobbying within the neighborhoods and a concerted get-out-the-vote effort on election day, all of which received extensive coverage in the *Idaho Statesman*. The annexation passed and the city made immediate plans to extend municipal services into the neighborhoods. Although a desire for amenities such as sidewalks, electricity and sewers motivated the citizens of Pleasanton and Ellis, a Progressive civics also animated their drive for inclusion in the greater city. Despite its youth and isolation, Boise participated in the new Progressive reform era of the United States in the first decades of the 20th century. Boise lacked many of the urban ills that drove reformers in the east, yet its citizens embraced the ideas of civic engagement and responsibility that grew out of the movement. During this period, Boise began concerted efforts to pave roads, build sidewalks and sewers and extend electricity and water lines into its neighborhoods, and the majority of the citizens willingly paid the taxes necessary to make it all happen. Boise also embarked upon its ambitious tree-planting project, driven largely by private citizens and service clubs, the success of which led to the desert city's later appellation as the "City of Trees." Civic participation, beautification and improvement inspired the growing population of Boise, who aspired to a city on a cultural and aesthetic level with any in the country. Although still a suburb, Pleasanton, and its neighbors to the north and south, no longer idealized a rustic, rural mode of living. Urban and urbane, Pleasanton began the process of bringing the suburbs into the city.

After 1910, Boise's explosive growth began to taper off, ending the first phase of suburban growth. In 1910, Hester Davis platted the remaining portion of her lands into the Frank Davis Addition, just west of Pleasanton across 27th. That same year, real estate developers platted the former farmlands west of Davis' holdings into the Hubbell Home Addition. As growth dropped off, so did sales of rural lots, and each addition remained unimproved and outside of the city limits until later in the century. With Boise's population interested in proper neighborhoods with standard amenities, Frank Davis and Hubbell Home could not compete with the established additions closer in. Despite a few sales and homes built, each addition remained largely empty until later in the century, when Frank Davis, like western West Side, filled in primarily with low-income housing and apartment complexes. A few homes were built on Hubbell Home's eastern edge of Rose Street, but the addition remained entirely vacant until the State of Idaho purchased it in the mid-1960s to build the new Transportation Department headquarters.

The slower growth rate brought about a consolidation of the established West End neighborhoods. With infrastructure in place and many lots
available, the West End, like later additions in the North and East Ends, filled
in steadily from the 1910s through the 1930s. Once established, the three

Todd Shallat

Pleasanton's vernacular mix of Craftsman Bungalows, Mission Revivals and
Italianate Picturesque recalls the streetcar era.

additions that constituted the core West End—Fairview, West Side and
Pleasanton—filled in with homes and urban amenities. Even as overall growth
in Boise slowed over the next 20 years, population and home building
increased in the West End. By the beginning of World War II, the West End
enjoyed full sewer, electricity and water utilities, paved streets and, east of
27th Street, sidewalks. Two neighborhood schools served the area, as did a
neighborhood store on 27th. Growth over time resulted in an attractive mix
of residential and commercial architecture. In the Pleasanton Addition, street
names were changed to reflect the distinct geography of the West End, even
as the city adjusted the street numbering system in order to standardize the
neighborhoods with the greater city. Though industrial and heavy

commercial uses persisted on the south and western edges, development of the core West End from 1910 through the mid-century created an urban residential neighborhood equal to, yet unique from, the North and East Ends.

Boise's post-World War II patterns of transit and suburban development shaped the fate of the West End in the latter half of the 20th century. Even as the residential center grew and stabilized from the 1910s to the 1940s, State Street to the north and Fairview to the south became major highways. After 1928, with the closing of the Boise streetcar, 27th Street became a major traffic corridor itself, connecting the two thoroughfares. Main Street, just north of Fairview, evolved into the westbound half of a couplet with Fairview, which moved traffic east. Main and Fairview, and State west of 23rd Street shifted further to commercial development, particularly that which oriented toward automobile traffic. Gas and service stations, hotels and motels, drive-through restaurants, banks and car dealerships sprang up along all three roads. These streets, with freight trains still running on the tracks to the south and the ongoing quarrying interests working to the west, hemmed in the West End with traffic, commerce and industry, and effaced its intact historical identity, even as the residential center maintained its integrity.

Today, the West End is not officially classified as a historic neighborhood, but it occupies a unique and important place in the city's past. When the suburbs that are now known as the "30th Street Area," among other names, were first platted, Boise was growing out of its origins as a rough frontier town into a city whose citizens believed themselves capable of building a modern civic community the equal of other great cities in the West. The West End reflected that ambition. The area of the city that constitutes Boise's historic first western suburbs remains a neighborhood whose development played a significant role in the city's maturing civic growth in the early 20th century. As a new suburban form accessible to a range of classes, and as an indicator of the increasingly sophisticated self-image of Boiseans and their aspirations, the West End shaped and reflected the growth of the city during a crucial era of its history.

• • •

Tully Gerlach began his West End research as the graduate "City Historian" for the Boise City Department of Arts and History. He received a BA in history in 1995 and a master's of applied historical research from Boise State University in 2010.

Idaho State Historical Society

Fast-growing Kuna began as a rail stop on the Union Pacific's Oregon Short Line. Pictured: raising the flag at the tent that held Kuna's first public school, 1909.

Catching up with

KUNA

by Jessica Lane

K una was first established in 1882 as little more than a dusty stop on the Oregon Short Line Railroad. Nothing then in the sparse settlement yielded a clue that it would eventually evolve into an agricultural oasis anchored by a city with subdivisions sprawling across what was once southwest Idaho desert. Until the recent housing crash, Kuna was in the throes of a frontier-style land rush. And local leaders are braced for even more growth once the market again turns bullish. But without the railroad's presence at the outset, Kuna may never have gained a foothold in its harsh environment. The settlement began after railroad managers in the East bypassed Boise, thinking its location along the Boise River was impractical for a railroad. Instead, Oregon Short Line workers laid tracks 15 miles to the south and built a small station house at a spot they would name "Kuna," a Native American word supposedly meaning "the end."

News of the station's location along Indian Creek was ill received by Boise's leaders and citizens, who felt that the stop at least should have been called Boise Station, despite its distance from the city. Leaders feared that freight shippers and businessman in other states wouldn't do business with the city if they didn't know what or where Kuna was. They carried their protest in 1883 to the opinion pages of the local newspaper, *The Idaho Tri-Weekly Statesman*. Led by editor Milton Kelly, the paper published a series of articles in September of 1883 ranting against what he considered the "ugliest, nonsensical name that could be picked out of Indian jargon for a railway station." The bitterness reflected Boise's keen disappointment that the railroad they had longed for was situated 15 miles away and carried a name that did not reflect the importance of their city. The first train reached Kuna Station on September 25, 1883. From there, supplies were transported by wagon to Boise or the mining camps of Idaho City and Silver City. Rail passengers could take a stagecoach to Boise or continue on to Winnemucca, Nevada. The small station served as Boise's main rail connection until the Idaho Central Railroad laid track between Nampa and Boise in 1887. That September, Kuna Station was closed and its brief existence as a railroad town came to an abrupt halt.

The name Kuna stuck, however, and soon came to be a reference for the area surrounding the former station house. Kuna gained a renewed sense of purpose when the F.H. Teed family filed a 200-acre claim for settlement in 1904 and later opened a post office. The Teed homestead was later sold in 1909 by lottery and became the town site for Kuna. Settlers had to travel to the Snake River for their water source, but in 1909 a well was dug after the Bureau of Reclamation provided $16,000 in bonds to finance the drilling. That same year, builders finished work on Arrowrock Dam and the New York Canal and thousands gathered to watch water flow from the canal to its destination in Lake Lowell near Nampa. Completion of these systems meant an inexpensive and readily available water supply for enterprising settlers. With water flowing, promoters mounted a campaign to attract additional settlers. Midwest businessman D.R. Hubbard issued an open invitation in national newspapers calling for enterprising individuals to "have a part in the building of a city." He advertised that 35,000 irrigable acres within five miles of Kuna were available for settlement, describing the new paradise as a "town site on a beautiful plateau overlooking the canal and depot grounds, with an outlook that charms all who see it" and promising that the development of the town would be an "incredible opportunity."

By 1912, Kuna contained a blacksmith shop and the first homesteaders were clearing the land for homes and businesses. At the time, Kuna was little more than a small agricultural community with a few families making up the general population. In 1916, Lucy Teed, one of homesteader F.H. Teed's

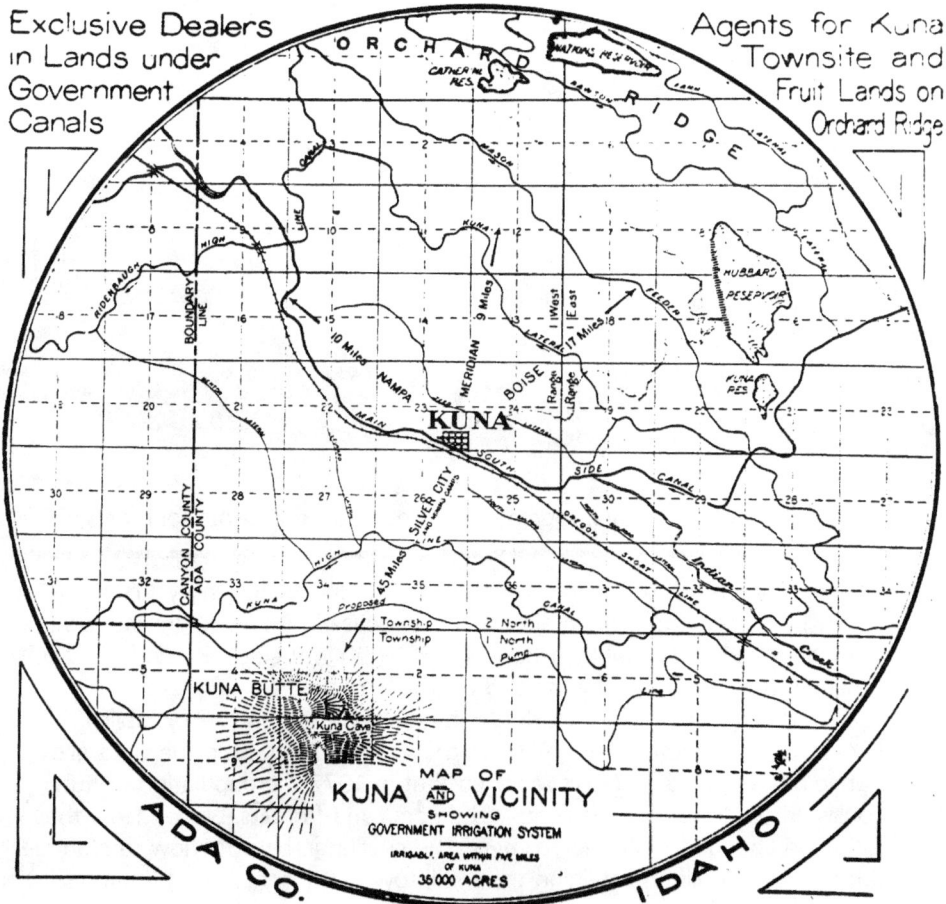

Kuna promoter D.R. Hubbard sold farmsteads with water from the New York Canal, 1909.

daughters, wrote about her experiences as a Kuna pioneer. She boasted that by 1916 Kuna had seen great success as an incorporated town with a population of 250, sanded streets, electric lights and power, an accredited school, multiple churches, a bank, newspaper, physician, post office, two general stores, a hotel, a barber and many other amenities—a remarkable

Idaho State Historical Society

Frank Fiss built Kuna's first mercantile store in 1909. City lots sold for $100.

accomplishment in such a short period of time. In the ensuing years, Kuna slowly built itself into a town almost solely focused on agriculture. Kuna's population remained stable at between 500-600 in the 1950s and '60s. Then it nearly tripled to 1,767 by the end of the 1970s.

The first concerns about Kuna's rapid expansion and sustainability began to surface in the late 1970s as growth was surpassing the city's economic base. The *Valley News* reported that in 1972 the population of Kuna consisted of almost 100 percent "old timers" and farmers, but by 1979 the ratio had changed to 2-1 newcomers. The challenge became how to manage rapid growth while maintaining the small town atmosphere that Kuna residents cherished. Duane Yamamoto, the mayor at that time, declared that "growth is unstoppable," but that the city hoped to preserve its rural atmosphere while coping with issues like inadequate water and sewer systems, additional police protection and expansion of the business district. Kuna's growth stabilized in the 1980s as the town held steady at about 2,000 residents. Then homeowners discovered Kuna. Fueled in part by migration from Ada and Canyon counties, population in the 1990s tripled to more than 6,000 and then more than doubled in the next 10 years to reach 16,100 in 2010. More than 60 percent of Kuna's homes were built between 2000-07.

Library of Congress HABS/HAER

The U.S. Reclamation Service, founded in 1902, remade West Ada County with well-engineered irrigation canals. Pictured: canal building near Kuna, 1907.

The city limits now envelop more than 17 square miles, a jump of 14 square miles over the last six years as the city annexed several new developments. Kuna now reaches the boundaries of Meridian and its subdivisions spread to within four miles of Boise, expansions of territory that have led to jurisdictional disputes with Kuna's neighbors.

With a surge of population coming to southwest Idaho from other states, Steve Hasson, director of Kuna's Planning and Zoning Department, believes many people prefer Kuna because they can build on cheaper land but remain close to amenities in Ada County such as the airport, major industry and Boise State University. Other areas of Ada County have placed limits on where development can still occur. As city planner Troy Behunin explained, "Developers cannot go toward the Foothills and cannot go east or north, so Kuna becomes a logical choice with its affordable land and a city that is welcoming any and all development."

Kuna continues to face the challenges a large populace brings. "As a city begins to grow and develop, so do its needs," said Mayor Scott Dowdy.

Larry Burke

The Kuna School District has added new schools to accommodate growth. Construction is well underway on the latest, Silver Trail Elementary.

With an increasing population, the demand also rises for infrastructure like water supplies, roads and schools. Kuna is in a constant race to keep up, and the city is responding with a variety of measures designed to enhance services. In 1998, for example, the city spent more than $2.5 million to expand its water and sewer system. The expansion was intended to handle six years of growth but barely lasted for three. In 2005, Kuna issued a moratorium on building permits because the city had once again run out of space for sewage pumping equipment and local sewer ponds were in violation of county odor requirements. The city recently completed a water and sewer treatment facility that includes 13,000 hookups to accommodate new development. But then growth stopped, and area landowners who formed a local improvement district to build the water system found themselves in a financial bind. Thinking their land would be more valuable with sewer connections, 59 landowners agreed to have their property assessed to pay off a loan to build the new system. When the market disappeared in 2007, they were left with huge assessments but had no way to sell their land to raise

Land for sale is still plentiful in Kuna, and 21st century homesteaders are encouraged to bring their own builders.

the money. Some faced foreclosure. The city agreed to pay a small portion of the loan; meanwhile, some property owners are contesting the assessments and the validity of the local improvement district in court.

Transportation is another concern as increasing numbers of drivers funnel onto area roads each day. Kuna hopes the eventual widening of the Meridian-Kuna Road and the opening of the new Interstate interchange at Ten Mile will improve traffic flow to and from Kuna. Collector roads are impacted most by growth, said Ada County Highway District Commissioner John Franden. "Existing roads have carried the growth, but in time we will have to widen them." The highway district has already installed stoplights at several intersections on the Meridian-Kuna Road to regulate the flow of high-speed traffic.

Kuna schools mirror community growth, with enrollment doubling over the past 10 years to the current 5,000 students, according to Jay Hummel, who has been involved with the district for 30 years as a patron, principal and now, superintendent. "When I was hired the board chair asked me, 'Is there any way you could possibly hang on to the great things about the small Kuna we all love while we are growing way too fast?' That is a challenge we all face," said Hummel. District patrons stepped forward to help in 2007 by approving a $25 million bond to build an alternative high school, classrooms and an auditorium at the high school and a new elementary school, Silver Trail, that will open in 2011. "The new elementary will help us ... we'll be OK for at least five years if the growth rate right now continues," said Hummel, who explained that enrollment growth now is 2-3 percent annually compared to 6-8 percent before the housing market cooled. One of

Larry Burke

After annexing several subdivisions, Kuna, with its familiar water tower, has expanded its city limits from 3 to 17 square miles since 2005.

Hummel's biggest growth-related concerns is student safety during the busy morning commute when as many as 2,000 students walk to school. "People leaving for work and kids going to school at the same time is a huge issue for us," he said.

As far as the city is concerned, continued growth is very much welcome. The city and its officials are gearing up to be ready to "rock and roll anywhere in the community," Hasson said. Despite the slow economy, home construction in Kuna continued to surge when most cities experienced a stagnant market. Building permits for single-family homes in 2008 jumped more than 12 percent over the previous year. And fueled in part by the first-time homebuyer credit, the city saw a spike in requests for building permits during three months in 2009. Kuna is eager to spread the word that the city is "business friendly." Fewer rules and regulations is one of the selling points the city emphasizes. For example, to hasten the construction of a new Walgreens Drug Store, the city quickly approved special-use permits over a three-month time frame. The national chain decided to move its construction schedule up 9 months. The city intends to develop a stronger commercial sector that will enhance local businesses, add local jobs and diversify the local tax base. Kuna supports between 1,000-1,200 jobs. "Currently, Kuna is lacking a strong economic foundation. The city is primarily a bedroom community to Boise. Most Kuna residents commute to other cities for work and return to Kuna to sleep," said Mayor Dowdy. More than 12,000 Kuna residents leave the city for work, with an average commute time of 26 minutes. A vibrant local economy, anchored by more national businesses, will accelerate the transition from commuter to full-fledged community. Commercial and retail operations need "sufficient rooftops" in order to consider building in an area. As Walgreens and a new Les Schwab tire store illustrate, national companies are beginning to eye Kuna because they see a growing population that is in need to services.

Long-term solutions are needed before Kuna outgrows itself any further. The city spent $250,000 over a three-year period to analyze its water systems and fundamental services, update population projections and present solutions for changing growth patterns. The city issued a new Comprehensive Plan in 2009. More than 300 pages, the plan is an official policy document to guide future development within city limits and the area of impact over the next 20 years. The city will use the document when preparing project plans, reviewing development proposals and adopting land use and transportation ordinances. The city also updated its land use map in 2009 and the new version will serve as a blueprint for future growth. "We had a tremendous turnout for our map overhaul, and are confident that it truly reflects the city's wishes and what is best as a whole," explained planner Behunin.

With Kuna evolving into a more family-oriented community, some have called for more open discourse with the city to ensure that citizens' needs are being met. Concerned residents like former New York businessman John Lamanna are part of grassroots efforts to encourage the community to become involved in the planning the city's future. "Kuna, while growing, can still be seen as somewhat backward and suffers from being surrounded by larger, more established cities," he said. Rather than follow in the footsteps of Meridian or Eagle, Kuna wants to forge its own identity while looking at a long-term vision, said Mayor Dowdy. "Change is coming to the valley whether we like it or not. Embrace it or get sucked into it unprepared. The fact is, the valley is a magnet for growth." Kuna continues to welcome

AshtonChris

In 2008 the city approved a 3,400 acre annexation that increased the size of Kuna by 50 percent. Pictured: vanishing farmland in West Ada County.

growth, but plans to keep its roots in agriculture and preserve open spaces to provide "ventilation" between other cities. However, there is now more of a market for "houses instead of corn" and economics will drive many of the growth decisions.

Kuna's proximity to two popular tourist attractions could enhance the city's long-term stability. Kuna is a gateway to the Birds of Prey National Conservation Area and the Western Heritage Historic Byway. The conservation area is home to the largest concentration of nesting raptors in North America. Its rich ecosystem supports 15 different raptor species and a variety of animals. The area also holds significant value from a cultural standpoint. Human presence dates back about 10,000 years. Large boulders washed in the canyon by the Bonneville Flood feature an array of petroglyphs and numerous archaeological sites are within the conservation area. The historic byway begins in Kuna and continues over 40 miles to Swan Falls Dam, the first hydroelectric project on the Snake River. The route provides access to historic and natural sites such as the Snake River Canyon and some of the best-preserved areas of the Oregon Trail. The continued protection and support of these lands could mean an increase in tourism—and a much-needed boost to Kuna's economy. Effective management of the open spaces around the city also could lead to a stronger economic base. Kuna's primary heritage lies in its agricultural roots. The first homesteads were built on farms and more than 100 years of successful agricultural tradition has followed. Beets, grain, wheat, beans, mint and corn are a few of the crops cultivated near Kuna. Proper management and protection of agricultural lands will ensure that prime agrarian and ranching locales remain important to Kuna's historic function as a city.

The 2009 Comprehensive Plan sheds light on the possibilities that lie in store for the small agricultural community that evolved from a controversial station house. At first glance, Kuna may seem like nothing more than the mirror image of any other mid-sized town in America. However, Kuna is the result of a unique historical background and geographical place. Whether one views Kuna's growth in a positive light or remains skeptical of "excessive" development, it is clear that the city cannot stand still. Change is very often an uncomfortable and costly process. Can Kuna's bullish approach to growth be sustained in the face of a recovering economy and increasing competition from other cities? Only time will tell. Regardless, it is important for residents to take an active role to create a community that develops in the ways the citizenry desires and to maintain its small-town ambiance in the face of continued growth. Just as in the homesteading days of D.R. Hubbard, there is an opportunity once again to be a part in the "building of a city" in Kuna.

· · ·

Jessica Lane is seeking a BA in history with an emphasis on the American West, with graduation anticipated in Fall 2012. She plans to pursue a master's degree in public history for a career in historical writing.

Jason Densmer/Flickr

Hidden Springs began with a master plan for 850 homes on 1,756 acres. Defenders call it sustainable smart growth. Critics say the community aggravates sprawl.

Hidden
SPRINGS
by Peter Thomas

To Treasure Valley residents, the name "Hidden Springs" holds a conspicuous place amongst its brethren. While names like "Bridge Tower" and "Lakemoor" certainly don't burden the ear, nor do they evoke the mental image that Hidden Springs does. Hidden Springs is a planned Smart Growth community in unincorporated Ada County, situated in the foothills approximately four miles north of the western edge of Boise. Whether the reaction is: "That's the planned community thing up in the hills, right?" or "Oh, you mean Pleasantville? Yeah, it's actually not bad up there," area residents seem to have at least some basic conception of the development. The feature that truly differentiates Hidden Springs is neither its "hilly-ness," nor its "pleasantvalley-ness," but rather its Smart Growthy-ness.

As the first Smart Growth development in the region, Hidden Springs' design, approval and construction processes were atypical. It did not physically resemble the subdivisions that were rapidly becoming a ubiquitous feature of the late 1990s as they spread into what was previously farmland. Perhaps more unusually, it was designed with the specific intent to create

Eva Hoops/Hidden Springs

Realtors call Hidden Springs "a true community" where neighbors interact. Pictured: Hidden Springs Fourth of July kiddie parade.

and foster a sense of community and identity that would be distinctly "Hidden Springs." Further, the design included ways to provide services—such as education, fire and mail—from within the community. Today, 12 years after the first houses were built, the current state of Hidden Springs is a useful example for identifying the effectiveness of policy decisions and design elements. It is the future, however, that will determine whether the Smart Growth ideals there are fully realized. Smart Growth principles aim to influence land use policies and development strategies to create more vibrant communities that reduce the number of vehicle miles that people travel daily and use less energy than more sprawling communities. Specific problems that conflict with that theme include the overextension of resources and infrastructure through sprawl and the loss of "sense of place" that has been associated with sprawl and urban decay. Smart Growth provides a comprehensive plan for creating such communities, including high-density housing, mixed-use planning and pedestrian-friendly neighborhoods. It is evident that these ideals guided the design of Hidden Springs.

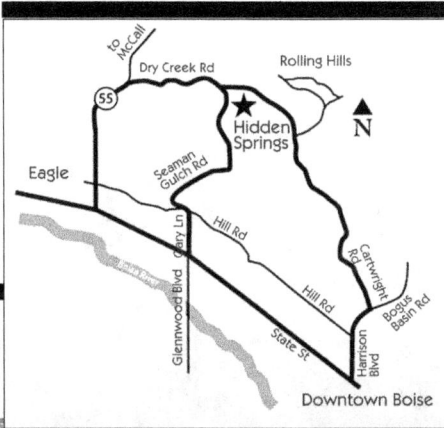

Hidden Springs is the brainchild of developer Jim Grossman. An Idaho native and Colorado College graduate, Grossman moved back home to Ketchum to become a ski instructor at the Sun Valley Resort before joining the family property development com-

Frank Lundburg/Flickr

Hidden Springs sits in Dry Creek Valley about 10 minutes from State Street and 20 minutes from downtown Boise.

pany. After working in Arizona, he returned to Idaho in the early 1990s and began to design Hidden Springs. When asked about his plans, Grossman told the *Idaho Statesman* that, "Money isn't driving this. As important as it is, it is equally important to create something that is different and new and that hopefully enriches the lives of people that make their home out there." Rather than simply building another subdivision of cookie-cutter homes, Grossman wanted to create a community. That notion is still present in Hidden Springs today. In the official welcome letter, it states, "The most

The Dry Creek Mercantile, or "Merc" as the locals call it, houses a café, post office, and general store. The developer sparked controversy in 2007 with a proposal to sell the store to the homeowners, using open-space preservation funds.

valuable amenity is the friendly and caring residents who call this area home." To many, the notion of community has been lost in contemporary American suburbia, where the car is the primary means of transportation. Community is essentially non-existent when people leave their garage at 7 a.m. and return at 6 p.m., and contact with neighbors is an irritating intrusion on personal time in front of the television. Grossman told the *Idaho Statesman* that he "envisioned a place where people sat on front porches and talked with neighbors and residents caught up on gossip at the general store. A community where the environment and open space were respected, and home businesses and rental units attached to houses were encouraged."

To Grossman, creating a sense of community meant having an old-fashioned "town center" as a central gathering place for community events, business and shopping. One design element of the "town center" is a central mailroom. Rather than using traditional mailboxes, residents come into contact with their neighbors. The mailroom is located next to an establishment called the "Merc" where locals can pick up basic necessities, coffee, drinks and food. Nearby is a public space designed for community events such as concerts and farmers' markets. These locations were integral to Grossman's concept of public interaction. Aside from simply having an old-fashioned town center and usable public space, designing a community meant creating an identity. Part of this identity lay in the architectural style of the town area, which, according to Idaho architect Charles Hummel (and designer of the Hidden Springs Fire Station), is definitely identifiable as both "Western" and "Idaho," and has style elements similar to town centers like Ketchum and Gooding. This also very distinctly embodies concepts found in the Congress for the New Urbanism, whose ideals are similar to Idaho Smart Growth. According to its charter, "[a]rchitecture and landscape design should grow from local climate, topography, history and building practice." By incorporating elements of "Idaho-ness," such as a weathered wooden pasture fence and an old-fashioned town center, Hidden Springs provides residents with a sense of identity that is often lost in many subdivisions that are indistinguishable from one another. Hidden Springs is Intermountain West; it is Idaho ... it wouldn't pass as Southern California or Maine.

Incorporating architecture that recalls old Idaho city centers addresses another primary concern of Smart Growth. Because these old city centers preceded the automobile, they were designed to be accessible and comfortable to pedestrians. Needless to say, most streets today, as automobile-friendly streets, tend not only to be uncomfortable to walk down, but also may be simply unsafe. No land developer can force people to walk, but Hidden Springs incorporates physical design elements intended to promote walking to and from the public spaces. Features such as narrower streets make a major impact by both slowing traffic and leaving room for more spacious sidewalks, including a grass barrier between the sidewalk and the street. Planters and landscaping further insulate pedestrians from the sound and stress of traffic. Finally, some form of shade, whether from trees or awnings, increases comfort for pedestrians. Hidden Springs' design reflects a conscious effort to include these kinds of elements to create a pedestrian-friendly street. In addition, parking space is limited to both encourage walking and maximize public space.

Pedestrian-friendly streets lose much of their charm in the absence of a meaningful public community space. The Merc/mailroom and adjacent park are unquestioningly the center of public space in Hidden Springs, whose design has, in fact, had an impact on the sense of "community" found there. Many residents feel at ease letting their school-age children ride their bikes, knowing that everyone keeps an eye out for one another. The Hidden Springs website offers a summer swim club for children, a list of teenage babysitters and informal social groups ranging from playgroups for toddlers to cooking groups for adults. This level of self-driven community involvement does not exist by accident. It is an intentional counter-reaction to sprawl, where large lot tract houses separate neighbors from traditional opportunities for interpersonal contact. A true sense of community has another great benefit. As people return to socializing and spending more time with their neighbors, they begin to connect with their physical environment and take responsibility for keeping it attractive and pleasant. This has traditionally been accomplished through covenants, conditions and restrictions set by neighborhood groups. Designers and architects, however, have begun to incorporate design elements that encourage people to proactively maintain the environment. Hidden Springs strives to keep up a pleasant appearance in both ways. Like many other neighborhoods, old and new, it has a comprehensive set of codes and restrictions regarding house appearance and other subjects. Hidden Springs, however, has gone further in encouraging people to care about their community by creating a sense of "place."

A primary cause of the loss of place is the rise of undifferentiated houses placed among cul-de-sacs in the midst of large subdivisions. People tend not to feel personally connected to neighborhoods that have no identifiable characteristics aside from different street names. In creating neighborhoods people care about, along with a sense of identity and place, it is a designer's job to understand what specific design elements resonate with people in any specific place. Grossman built on the lessons he learned as a child in Ketchum about the notion of a town center and used architecture familiar to him to re-create the feel of early Idaho downtown buildings. Additionally, the houses themselves are brightly colored and are definitely distinct from the prefabricated beige houses that were popular at the time Hidden Springs was started. Another feature of the houses is that their design recalls pre-automotive neighborhoods, with large porches, small front yards and garages located in the rear of the house. These specific elements are designed to further increase community interaction.

At the outset, preservation of open space was a prominent feature of the design. In total, of the 1,884 acres in the development, the *Statesman* reported that between 810 and 900 [were] to remain permanent open space designated as farmland, natural space and wildlife preserves. By promoting dense housing developments, an abundance of open space became available for public use. In addition, a community farm was started as a way to preserve farming and rural traditions in Hidden Springs. While the farm had existed for nearly a century and a half, it was certainly not a foregone conclusion that it would remain. Around 100 acres, it provides residents

Gavin J. King

Hidden Springs features more than 800 acres of open space and expansive views of the foothills.

access to organically grown vegetables as well as a way to actively partici-pate in the process. As residents find use for the open space, the likelihood that they will take an interest in its upkeep increases. On the Hidden Springs website, residents are encouraged to "participate in community cleanups, pick up a bit of litter while you walk and avoid muddy or wet trails." To pro-vide ongoing source of funds, a transfer tax where a percent of a home's sales price, paid by the seller, is devoted to a preservation account managed by a nonprofit conservation association.

Idaho Smart Growth and the Congress for the New Urbanism promote mixed-use development as one way to reduce automobile commuting. Trends in the 20th century leaned toward the separation of commercial, resi-dential and industrial districts within a municipal area. Compounded by the mass ownership of the automobile and the relative convenience of the

In 2000 the National Association of Homebuilders awarded Hidden Springs its Platinum Award for Smart Growth. In 2010, home prices ranged from about $140,000 to $750,000.

Interstate Highway System, different areas of usage may be significant distances apart. It is not uncommon for people in large metropolitan areas to commute up to two hours to and from work every day. Incorporated into Hidden Springs is the concept of mixed-use design, which New Urbanism defines as the "concentration of civic, institutional and commercial activity...embedded in neighborhoods and districts." In other words, neighborhoods should provide basic essentials such as housing, food, employment, education and recreation within walking or biking distance. This greatly reduces the negative impact of mass automobile transit and its supporting infrastructure. Jim Grossman's concept was to build a mixed-use community outside of Boise in a manner that would greatly reduce the amount of automobile use necessary for the residents. A significant amount of space near the front of the development is intended for commercial usage. Ideally, the most efficient use of that space would be businesses that provided services and employment to residents. Closely related to the inclusion of mixed use in a development is attracting a socioeconomically and culturally diverse population. The term commonly used is "affordable housing," which is not synonymous with subsidized or low-income housing. The implication of having a mixed-use community where people can walk or bike to work is that there will be a diversity of income levels. While dentists, doctors and executives make an attractive potential market for developers, the idea of mixed use cannot be realized in a community without cooks, teachers and janitors. In order to reduce automobile use and commute times, it is vital to provide affordable housing to all community members. Ideally, according to the Idaho Smart Growth guiding principles, "neighborhoods should offer a range of options: single-family homes—duplexes, garden cottages and condominiums—and accommodations for dependent elders." Grossman's original ideal was to provide a mix of housing, so he designed three separate "neighborhoods"—The Village, The Valley and The Foothills—representing three different price levels, with lot prices at the time in The Village starting at around $45,000 and up to $214,000 in The Foothills.

Despite the bold concepts behind Grossman's development, Hidden Springs has had its share of struggles. As an Idaho Smart Growth board member and land use policy expert, Gary Allen is quick to note that Grossman was a dreamer, not a developer. The design seemed to be too "high end" and the development quickly ran into financial problems. Hidden Springs was returned to GMAC, a large mortgage company from whom Grossman Properties had borrowed. This was neither the beginning nor the end of struggles for Hidden Springs. From the early stages of development, it faced unique challenges in implementing its goals. With its new and untested design, Hidden Springs had to jump major hurdles to earn the approval of the Ada County Planning and Zoning Commission. Its design and function represented something new and untested in the area. One of the issues was how to provide services that were typically the provenance of governmental entities. Providing sewer treatment, for example, required the development to fund the physical infrastructure and maintenance, in addition to adopting a plan that adhered to strict state regulations. Police services, through the Ada County Sheriff's Department, needed to cover the construction site long before revenue would be generated by residents. Education, fire protection and emergency response, street lights and other basic services had to be cobbled together by an entity not accustomed to doing so.

Grossman's Smart Growth goals have not all been fully realized. While the website states that Hidden Springs "will offer a variety of homes so that people of many ages, incomes and backgrounds can live at Hidden Springs," it might be a stretch to argue that there is true socioeconomic diversity there. As a former teacher at Hidden Springs Elementary, William Waag got the impression that "It's almost as though the community screens potential residents before they were allowed in ... not only would I say that it is NOT diverse, but I think diversity of culture and values is almost exactly what the residents are trying to avoid." His assessment was that it seemed to be a popular location for upper-class businessman and doctors to raise their children outside the influence of lower socioeconomic classes and cultures. Addressing the lack of population diversity, Allen and Hummel both noted that there is a limit to "designing people's behavior." While there are varying levels of cost for lots, Hidden Springs was not necessarily designed to provide housing for people with moderate to low incomes, and as an "upper-middle class place," it may actually be less exclusive than the designers originally anticipated. Without the availability of affordable housing for individuals of average income, locating centers of employment in Hidden Springs is also a major challenge. A vast majority of working individuals commute to Boise every day. Without significant employment, it could be criticized simply as another example of urban sprawl, albeit a pleasant looking, expensive example. This fact directly conflicts with the design of Hidden Springs as at least a partially self-contained development. Despite Hidden Springs' proximity to Boise, the actual commuting distance is significant, and drivers must travel out of their way to reach the major arterials that service the Treasure Valley.

Key components of Smart Growth are missing from Hidden Springs. Some criticisms are aimed at the struggles that it has gone through financially, a lack of diversity, a minimal amount of employment and seemingly an increase in the traffic congestion on State Street and Hill Road. These hardly represent a sterling picture of Smart Growth in action. This invites the question: "Is Hidden Springs a failure?" In response, it is necessary to look at the larger context in which Hidden Springs exists. In analyzing Hidden Springs and its relation to Smart Growth, Gary Allen stressed that it is simply a component in a much larger picture. The future of Hidden Springs, and its

Critics call it "Pleasantville" in reference to the 1998 movie spoof of a too-perfect American suburb. Residents treasure their walkable streets with parks, community gardens and vintage architecture.

success as a Smart Growth community, has more to do with surrounding developments in the long term, perhaps a century or more. If land use policy and developers adopt and maintain Smart Growth ideals, then Hidden Springs will be an important part of that picture, explained Allen. Concerns take on a different light in a larger picture. Hidden Springs, from a policy and design standpoint, is a fundamental step in the right direction. A considerable amount of employment in the community requires a large business or several employers. To attract businesses requires reaching a threshold of population. At 1,000 homes, Hidden Springs falls far short of the threshold for a standard grocery store, which requires around 14,000 homes in its market area; even something as small as a restaurant may require as many as 3,000 homes. Should the proposed Dry Creek development adjacent to Hidden Springs generate another 3,000 homes for the market area, however, then the commercial space in Hidden Springs may start to become a viable place to consider opening a business. This, in turn, may lead to a demand for

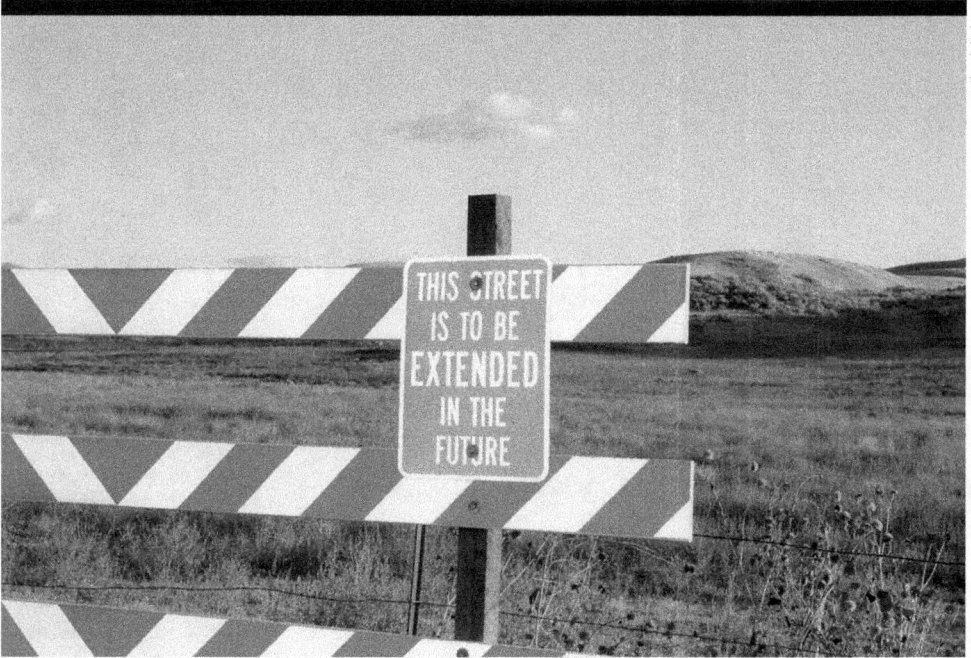

The Land Trust of the Treasure Valley works with the Hidden Springs Town Association to maintain a conservation easement. Homebuyers pay a "transfer fee" for a trail and open-space conservation fund.

affordable housing, which may not be in Hidden Springs, but may be located in a neighboring community.

As similar developments are designed and constructed, Hidden Springs provides an example of the process for implementing many Smart Growth ideals. Despite its obvious struggles, Hidden Springs is by no means a failure. It was constructed with no contemporary local or regional precedents of any type. After their new concept struggled through the approval process in the late 1990s, developers watched as their design was realized and did their best to dynamically adapt to specific concerns. Developers brought to fruition the idea of a more energy-efficient, dense urban space with usable, comfortable public space and pedestrian access. The state of Hidden Springs is summed up succinctly by Gary Allen: "Hidden Springs is as good as it could be, for what it is, but let's not make it something it's not." For any of its perceived successes and failures, it may realistically be too early to tell whether Hidden Springs will represent the beginning of a trend in housing developments, or if it will become nothing more than an oddity that nobody can quite figure out. Just as the measure for determining Hidden Springs' fate is time, so is it the measure for determining the fate of the Smart Growth principles that apply there. Smart Growth is more than just elements of architecture and design. It is more than lobbying groups and land-use policy. For Smart Growth to have the impact it desires, its ideals will have to transcend the Smart Growth label and instead represent "normal." In that process, Hidden Springs is a first step.

• • •

Peter Thomas is a senior studying political science with an emphasis on American government and public policy. He has been a resident of the Treasure Valley for 25 years, with family in Idaho for more than a century across many generations.

Bown Crossing's commercial zone uses Smart Growth concepts to create a pedestrian-friendly environment.

Urban

OASIS

by Jan Higgenbotham

Y ou are certain you have been here before. The doors to the shops are precisely the color you remember. Even the faces of the people and the whiff of the air seem recognizable. The place feels comfortable and safe. It feels like home. What generates this sense of experience with a place? What is it about a place that makes recognition more than déjà vu? Are there universal elements of "place" that sooth our souls regardless of our backgrounds, age or culture? Is it something that never goes away, never changes and continues to sustain us? Is it sustainable itself? By implementing New Urbanist concepts, Boise's Bown Crossing has captured the essence of place. By tapping into our collective memory of more compact urban spaces, the development supports sustainable growth and discourages sprawl.

New Urbanism favors narrow interconnected streets, open spaces, consistent compact blocks, buildings with the textures and colors of the landscape and neighborhoods designed to facilitate walking and biking, with short transit distances to work, shopping and recreation. New Urbanism

Larry Burke

In 1879, Joseph and Temperance Bown used Table Rock sandstone to build a two-story cupola "block house." Today the historic Bown House fronts Riverside School.

recalls a time when people lived closer to work and when a neighborly sense of place promoted well-being and pride. Community was important to Joseph and Temperance Bown when they built their farm home on the now Bown Crossing site southeast of Boise in 1879. In keeping with the popular Italianate architecture of the time, the house features a low-pitched roof and a blocky, rectangular shape with a square cupola on top. Quite opulent in comparison to the tents in which most families lived at the time, the Bown's home was built of darker-colored local sandstone from the Boise foothills on the front and lighter-colored, more common stone on the sides. Boise had

Bown Way connects Parkcenter Boulevard to Boise Avenue. Bown Crossing, opened in 2006, is a 36-acre tribute to New Urbanism with its compact mix of restaurants, shops, offices, townhouses and patio homes.

advanced from a mining and fur trading area to a farm community by the time the Bowns built their home on farmland far from the town center. In 1893, the Bowns sold their farm to W.T. Booth and moved to a farm to the west. It was a peaceful rural existence punctuated with quail hunting and swimming in the river. As time progressed, Boise became Idaho's center of government and industry. Changes in the nature of work affected how people traveled, where people lived and most importantly, how they interacted with and experienced their community. Functioning in the early 1900s as an employment and shopping core for the region, Boise featured a tight network of narrow streets, small building parcels and compact residential neighborhoods surrounding downtown. In time, the automobile not only became the symbol of prosperity, but also the primary mode of transportation. By the 1970s, Boise had developed an incoherent pattern of roadways leading to cul-de-sacs and disconnected streets, all designed to lessen the impact of car traffic in far-reaching neighborhoods of strangers. Suburban housing developments began to sprawl in all directions.

Boise was coming of age as an urban community about the time Peter O'Neill took a job with Boise Cascade in 1965. Having served on both the policy advisory board for the National Association of Homebuilders and the Harvard-MIT Joint Center for Urban Studies, he described that time as a confluence of country business acumen with the need for more precisely skilled professionals to evaluate and plan Boise's growth needs. O'Neill longed to one day find the right place and time to put his passion and vision for urban design to work, a place where the natural environment had not already been muddled by poor planning and development. That place turned out to be along the Boise River known as the "wrong side of town," down in the "flood plain." By 1979, O'Neill had started River Run Development Company, the predecessor of his current company, OE LLC, which acquired much of the 125 acres running along the south side of the river and out toward the ranch lands east of Boise. Over time O'Neill completed the River Run Master Plan for the entire area. In the mid-1980s, O'Neill started the River Run and Spring Meadow developments along Parkcenter Boulevard. By the late 1980s Ivan Harris was ready to sell his ranch, including the old Bown site. That decade's difficult economy and the heavy development expenses of bringing the River Run Master Plan to reality left O'Neill unable to make the purchase. "We drank a lot of lemonade and coffee sitting on the back porch getting to know one another in those days," O'Neill laughed. Finally, with the financial backing of long-time Pennsylvania investor Robert Kopf, the final few pieces running along Parkcenter Boulevard, including the Bown site, were purchased to complete the plan.

The Bown parcel had been identified as a commercial park in the master plan because of its proximity to an anticipated future bridge across the Boise River near a convergence point between Boise Avenue and Parkcenter Boulevard. With their headquarters just a few miles down the street and a vision of southeast Boise's future growth projections, the Albertsons grocery chain aggressively pursued Kopf to purchase this parcel. Eventually they succeeded and purchased the Bown parcel with an eye toward making the site a destination supermarket for the area. In the late 1990s, OE LLC developed Surprise Valley on a major piece of the Ivan Harris land further south and west from Bown. The prevailing subdivision design at the time, encouraged by market demand and anxiety over car traffic, included widespread use of cul-de-sacs and small loop-roads. These roads disconnected neighborhoods, forcing local trips onto increasingly congested arterial roads. River Run Drive

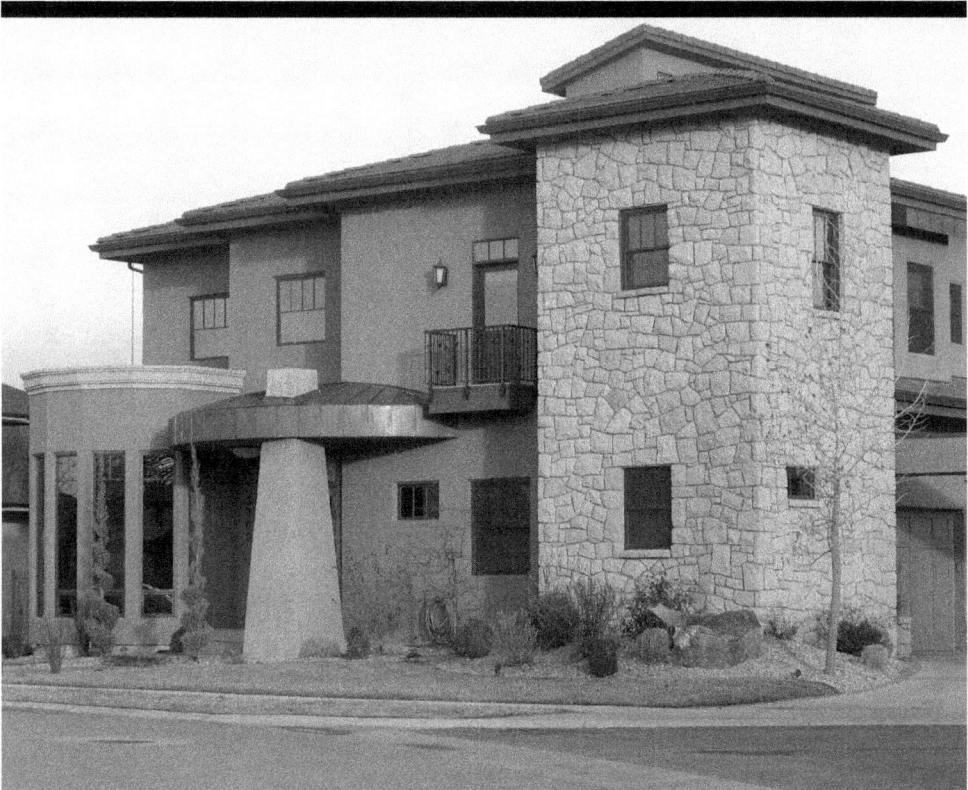

Larry Burke

Bown Crossing recalls the Italianate style of the original 1879 farmhouse. This 2006 Bown Crossing architectural showpiece mixes Italianate, Art Deco and International styles.

in River Run and Surprise Way in Surprise Valley provide examples of collector roads gathering traffic from the adjacent cul-de-sacs and circle drives. During this era, homes had at least two- and usually three-door garages facing the street. Neighborhood centers consisting of swimming pools, tennis courts and community halls were dedicated to resident use only and were often closed on nights and weekends. However, O'Neill had a different picture in mind for the old Bown farmstead. Inspired by Congress for the New Urbanism principles, he bought the Bown Crossing property back from Albertsons. With the help of citizens who wanted more school sites in southeast Boise, O'Neill traded some land to the school district to build Riverside

Larry Burke

Riverside Elementary School serves families in Bown Crossing and other east Boise neighborhoods. The school uses the Bown House as living museum to teach pioneer history.

School. The district's land acquisition included the Bown House, which was preserved and used for educational purposes. The final step to replacing an Albertsons supermarket as the area's traffic-generating anchor came when the City of Boise agreed to purchase part of the land for a future library site.

O'Neill envisioned the human need to replicate what we remember from childhood, the homes of our past. These are the places that recall the meaning and value of myths, something quite different from a neighborhood grocery store. Until the late 1990s, however, O'Neill described the planning process in Boise as encouraging simple lot and block "corn field" subdivisions. Zoning required wide collector streets and setbacks from the major arterials running traffic to and from the homes of the neighborhoods. "For some reason, bigger was seen as better," said O'Neill about home design. "There didn't seem to be an understanding that discretionary home buyers want various living situations that just have to be nice." At that time, smaller building parcels and homes were almost always of lower quality. He wanted Bown to be the new gold standard where everyone wanted to live, work and play, even though many of the homes and building sites were small.

By 1993, the City of Boise had hired Hal Simmons, now the planning director for the Planning and Zoning Department. One of his first projects was to update and rewrite the Boise Comprehensive Plan. Adopted in 1997, it was refined one year later by the addition of the pedestrian commercial zone, which became the foundation of mixed-use urban design in Boise. O'Neill, working with Simmons, was one of the first to utilize the new zone. At Bown Crossing, the zoning allows for office, residential and retail mixed uses. Convenient access to daily tasks minimizes traffic congestion and reduces visual clutter. Buildings correspond to the street on a pedestrian scale. Parking goes to the side and rear of the buildings. Derek O'Neill, Peter's son and president of O'Neill Enterprises, worked with the city and highway district to improve Bown Crossing's original plan. The southeast neighborhoods along Boise Avenue were joined with those of Parkcenter and Warm Springs Boulevards. Other concerns, such as moving and maintaining two irrigation arterials (thus mitigating risks of building below the elevation of the New York Canal), utilizing the land near the Riverside School as a transition zone between mixed-use commercial and residential development and providing right-of-way for the future East Parkcenter Bridge, were also addressed in a collaborative way. In the end, the City of Boise helped establish a prime example of New Urbanism in its approach to this commercial infill. Simmons called it a "fantastic model" that "benefits everyone within a mile or two."

In 1995, when *Newsweek* first reported on the Congress for the New Urbanism, journalist Jerry Alder seemed to anticipate Bown Crossing when he described several ways to fix the suburbs. Small lawns, street landscaping, pedestrian access to shopping, corner stores, skinny streets, gridded streets, hidden garages, varied housing types, a buffer of open space, small parking lots, low street lighting, a neighborhood center: these and other New Urbanist characteristics give Bown its sense of place.The development also receives high marks for its consistency with the city's Comprehensive Plan. It attempts to protect waterways and vegetation. It mixes residences with two- and three-story commercial buildings. Narrow streets now join previously disconnected but contiguous neighborhoods. Low-light street lamps recall the era of streetcar suburb. Trees add shade and texture, and sidewalks separate pedestrians from the bustle of cars. Bown Crossing also earned kudos for dispensing with street-clogging cul-de-sacs. Derek O'Neill said 33 percent of the 36-acre Bown Crossing site is open space that features connecting

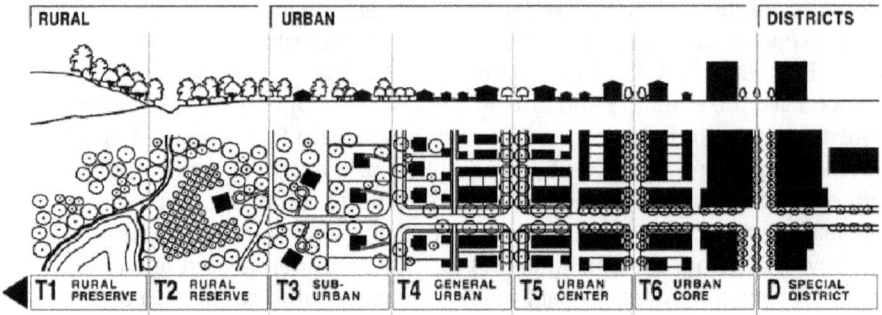

RURAL		URBAN				DISTRICTS
T1 RURAL PRESERVE	T2 RURAL RESERVE	T3 SUB-URBAN	T4 GENERAL URBAN	T5 URBAN CENTER	T6 URBAN CORE	D SPECIAL DISTRICT

Disciples of the New Urbanism strive for neighborhood densities that maximize consumer choice. This transect diagram shows the type of street, landscaping and building that is fits each environment, from the low-density rural to high-density urban.

pathways to the town square, neighborhood streets and the Greenbelt. Garages and the majority of parking remain behind buildings or tucked into the front exterior of homes. Condominiums, townhomes, patio homes, loft apartments and custom homes combine to offer a mix of living opportunities in a diverse price range of $217,000 to $1.3 million. Some of the residents work in the shops, restaurants and businesses in Bown Crossing. Others commute to work on bicycle, while retirees enjoy close access to the biking and hiking trails of Boise.

Even though the recent completion of the East Parkcenter Bridge improved the connectivity of Bown Crossing to outlying biking and walking paths, connections to public transit—the freeway, airport and across town—remain limited by access through adjacent neighborhoods along Boise Avenue and Parkcenter Boulevard. This disconnection with outlying transportation options affects the ability of residents and merchants within Bown Crossing to reduce their reliance on vehicle travel. On the other hand, Urban Land Institute research indicates that residents in compact developments like Bown travel 20-40 percent fewer miles compared to low-density developments and 60 percent less than urban neighborhoods.

The primary difference from other neighborhood centers developed in Boise is the town square. Bown residents can enjoy outdoor music, family night out, patio dining, block parties and a farmer's market right in the center of town. The new town center also reflects its heritage through its

Aaron Catt

Pouring foundations for the Riverwalk subdivision at Bown Crossing, the project's final residential phase, 2010. Homes are expected to start at $218,000.

architecture. The Bown family designed their farm home in the Italianate motif popular at the turn of the 20th century. Aaron Catt, of O2 Marketing Group located from Bown Crossing, describes O'Neill's design as incorporating this era quite well into Bown Crossing. An almost identical replica of the soffit of the Bown House is reflected in the commercial building housing a Mexican restaurant at the corner of Bown Way and Riverwalk Drive. The use of sandstone exteriors and exterior colors reminiscent of the Bown House have become part of the community, and street names like Bown Way, Abigail Way, Herbert Drive, Temperance Way and Rookery Lane preserve the memory of the Bown family and their time. Integrated into the Italianate architecture, O'Neill added similar aspects of California Bungalow and Craftsman design to unite texture and interest into the overall look of Bown Crossing. Tying the old with the new, O'Neill designed the town square to center on a view of the cupola of the Bown House.

Condominiums are among the mix of residential choices for residents in Bown Crossing.

According to Derek O'Neill, they conducted a combination of 72 public and neighborhood meetings during the planning and development process of Bown Crossing. During these meetings, neighbors and the city discussed concerns about connecting walking paths between Bown and existing neighborhoods to the east and north. The Ada County Highway District wanted a major connector between Parkcenter Boulevard and Boise Avenue to cross at Holcomb Road. O'Neill applied the outcomes of these discussions to the final version of the development. The highway district eventually discovered that a connector road twice as long as the one there now was not only cost-prohibitive, but it also would certainly disrupt the quaint nature of the current town square feeling of place. The new connector would not be the 'skinny' street that became the backbone of commerce and neighborly communion along its edges.

One of the amenities mentioned on several occasions by city officials and neighbors alike was the inclusion of a branch library at the site. Internal market studies conducted by O'Neill years before showed that libraries greatly enhance the well being of community inhabitants and fit well with New Urbanism design standards. While the city owns the land dedicated for a library at Bown Crossing, the first bond election necessary to raise funds to build the structures failed and the project is now on hold until funding is available.

New Urbanism place-making concepts—narrow streets, a variety of housing choices, hidden garages, protected waterways and connected neighborhoods—found a welcome home in Bown Crossing. Subsequent communities at 36th and Hill Road and the next phases of Harris Ranch look to the Bown model for reassurance and process modeling. In Peter O'Neill's mind, though, the key to designing New Urbanism communities is to focus on the right mix of uses. Using this approach, Bown Crossing benefitted the surrounding neighborhood, the city and everyone involved, while providing a local example to other developers of a New Urbanism design that works. Bown Crossing captured the essence of how place enhances the human experience by tapping into our collective memory. The Bown House provides a reminder of design tested by time. The partnership formed with the City of Boise and the citizens of the surrounding neighborhoods enhanced the outcomes for everyone as demonstrated by busy streets, a commercial center and owner-occupied homes at Bown Crossing, something of a novelty for communities built in the mid-2000s. The capability of O'Neill Enterprises to risk updating their successful designs in River Run, Spring Meadows and Surprise Valley to accommodate New Urbanism concepts in Bown Crossing, and rejecting sprawl, speaks of their desire to move Boise toward designs established when people and not automobiles drove the creation of communities with a sense of "place."

• • •

Jan Higgenbotham recently graduated from Boise State University with a degree in general studies and a minor in business, focusing on dispute resolution. She is an associate broker with Atova Real Estate and a certified professional mediator.

Idaho State Historical Society

Sisters of J.R. Field in his orchard in 1914. The Field farm is located at the bottom of Freezeout Hill near the present day Sanders Fruit Ranch.

Once there were
TREES

by Don Cutbirth

here was a time when a family would drive to Emmett in the spring-time just to see the fruit blossoms. It was a breathtaking sight of pink and white flowering trees. Along with their lush beauty, trees in bloom exude a sense of hope in us. The blooms somehow promise that, through their new beginning, our world will be made anew. In some way our spirits are lifted in trouble-free, childlike joy by the delightful specta-cle of blossoms skirting the Emmett Valley to the distant horizon. Today the landscape of the Emmett Valley is different. The drive on State Highway 16 to the rim of Freezeout Hill and down its steep slope reveals an impressive view. But it is a different view now. After more than 30 years of change, most of the fruit trees that once defined the valley below are gone. Emmett was once called the "Valley of Plenty" due to its rich soil and access to water. What was an agrarian community has become a suburban community of commuters. More than 50 percent of the Emmett households earn their living by working in the Boise-Meridian, Nampa-Caldwell, or Payette-Ontario areas. So, what happened to the fruit trees?

The early settlers to the Emmett Valley found the moderate climate and soil conditions ideal for growing fruit, which was used to supplement the family's diet. Surplus crops were sold to miners who craved fresh fruit and produce. With the extension of the railroad to Nampa and beyond, land developers started to advertise the valley's potential as far east as New York. By the 1890s, imaginative land developers realized that the valley's irrigation systems, then in their infancy, could open more sagebrush land to development, including fruit orchards. During those early years, real estate advertisements enticed many people who had the wealth and the strength of will to follow their dreams to Emmett. For many years the valley bloomed as farmers planted huge tracts of fruit trees that flourished for the next 80 years. Then the landscape began to change. Amendments to the Clean Air Act during the 1970s brought about major changes in the fruit orchard business. Farmers traditionally heated their orchards during the cold spring nights by burning fuel oil in rudimentary stoves called smudge pots. When these devices were not available, growers sometimes openly burned old automobile tires or coal in their orchards. This heating process raised the ambient temperatures and held back the damaging effects of the frost during the early morning hours until the sun came up to heat the valley. Smudging was an expensive operation. In some years, the costs of fuel oil and additional labor consumed the farmer's profits.

Air quality suffered whenever smudging took place. The smudge pots consumed thousands of gallons of oil, creating a huge oily black cloud of smoke that hung over the valley, especially in the early morning hours. But changes in the Clean Air Act put an end to smudging. After the practice was prohibited in the 1970s, orchard production, particularly in the lower, more frost-prone areas, became unreliable and economically unsustainable. Growers were forced to find alternative uses for their land. A common solution was to convert their property to other crops or pasture for livestock. Following the 1970s, some landowners found it advantageous to sell off portions of their property to housing developers. Out-of-state competition from Washington and other fruit producing areas had reduced the profitability for Emmett's orchardists. Changes in the produce distribution systems, which relied upon eastern buyers and brokers, reduced demand for Emmett's prune and plum producers.

Another economic incentive enticing Emmett farmers to sell their land for development has been the growing real estate market, along with the increasing number of people who want to live there. Gradually, much of

Gem County's farm and ranch land has been converted to residential property for a commuter population who works outside the county. In some cases,
land that once produced fruit has gone idle, been seeded to pasture or
reverted back to desert while waiting for a developer's offer to buy it.
Emmett Valley's population has increased over the past 40 years. Much of
this growth can be attributed to the development of new subdivisions and
individual houses on rural acreages. The force driving this development
relates both to economic concerns and to quality of life issues. People who
work for employers in Boise or other nearby cities find that housing costs in
the Emmett area are lower than those closer to their work. Those savings
offset the costs of commuting to work. The quality of life and small-town
atmosphere found in areas like Emmett have attracted many families. There
is a perception that the community offers a wholesome country life. Parents
see it as a good place to raise their children. Retired folks see it as a place to
live out their years for the same reasons.

The story of the Emmett Valley is one of hope and opportunity.
Beginning with the early settlers irrigating desert land and developing fruit
orchards, to the commuter community of today, people have worked for a
better life. Many of the orchards are gone and have been replaced by houses, asphalt and concrete. Bringing the trees back is no longer an option. The
springtime flowering orchards that once awakened our optimism for life
anew are a fading memory.

• • •

Don Cutbirth, an Emmett native, earned a BBA in finance from Boise
State University in 1974 and a master's of divinity from Southern
Methodist in 2001. He has completed coursework for an MS in
instructional & performance technology and plans to earn a certifi-
cate in conflict management.

Founded in 1883, platted in 1900, Emmett emerged as a way station between Boise and Baker City. Electricity and irrigation began to transform the valley after 1907. Pictured: Emmett Main street with buggies and automobiles on "Circus Day," 1910.

Fruit canning plant on the George Hall orchard near Emmett, 1914. The plant could produce 5,000 cans in a day.

Idaho State Historical Society

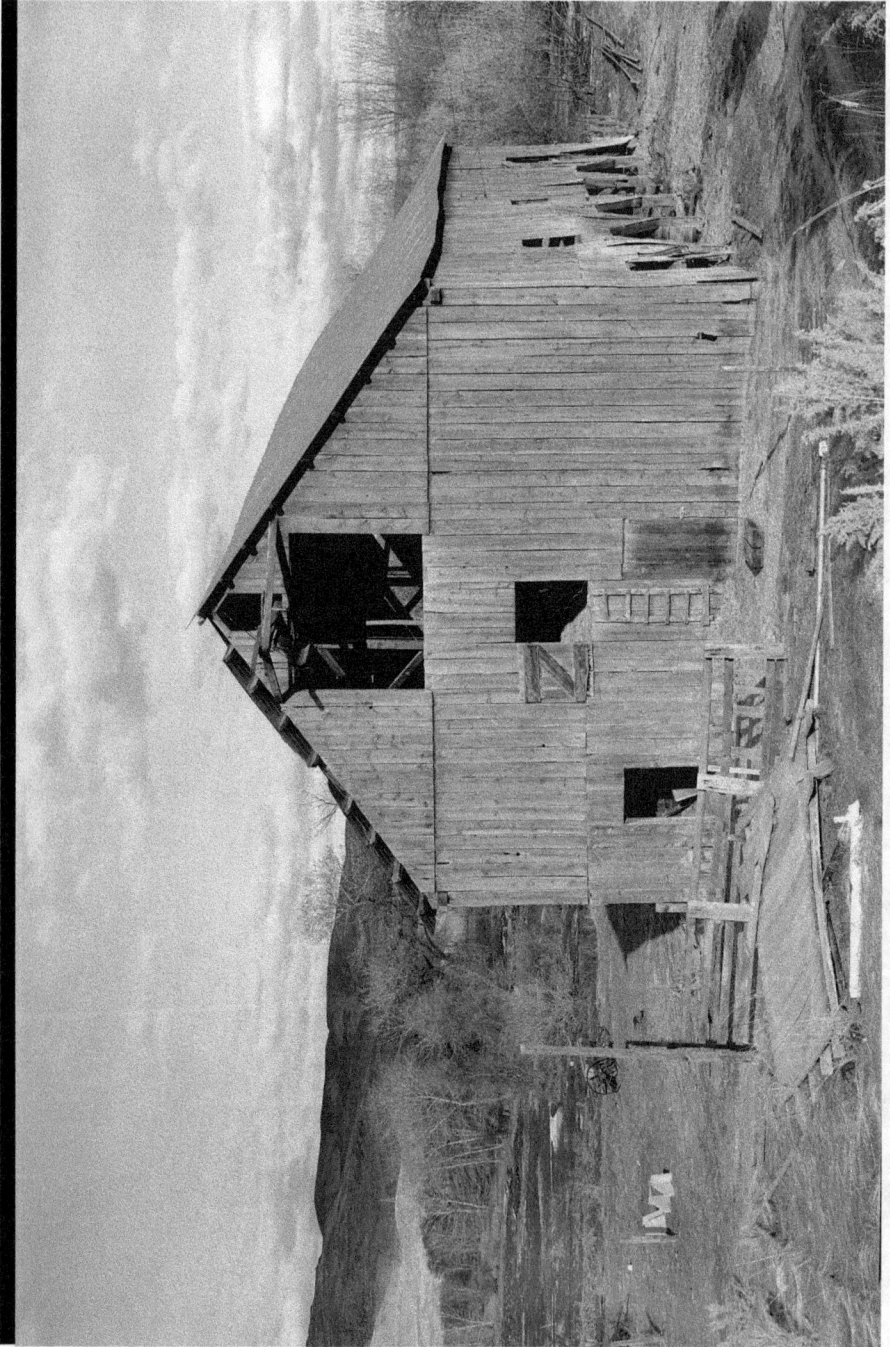

Plowman Sawmill above Emmett on the north bank of the Payette River. Built in 1896, the mill recalls an era of logging and mining that predated irrigated agriculture.

Works Progress Administration photographer Russell Lee contrasted the lushness of orchards in Emmett with the barren cut through Freezeout Hill, 1941

Cherry orchards beneath Emmett's Valley of Plenty, from a study by Russell Lee of the Works Progress Administration, 1941.

WPA/Library of Congress

Subdivisions pave over farmland in the Valley of Plenty between Squaw Butte and Freezeout Hill, 2008.

Phydeaux460/Flickr

Young farmer with tractor, Gem County, from a study of New Deal farming cooperatives by Dorothea Lange, 1939.

picturelinda/Flickr

Russell Lee reported that southern Idaho exported some 200 carloads of black cherries in 1941. Pictured: cherry orchard.

Paul Wicks/Flickr

Emmett's smudge pots were an import from the orange groves of Southern California after a bad freeze in January 1913. Federal regulations phased out Idaho smudging after the passage of the 1970 Clean Air Act amendments.

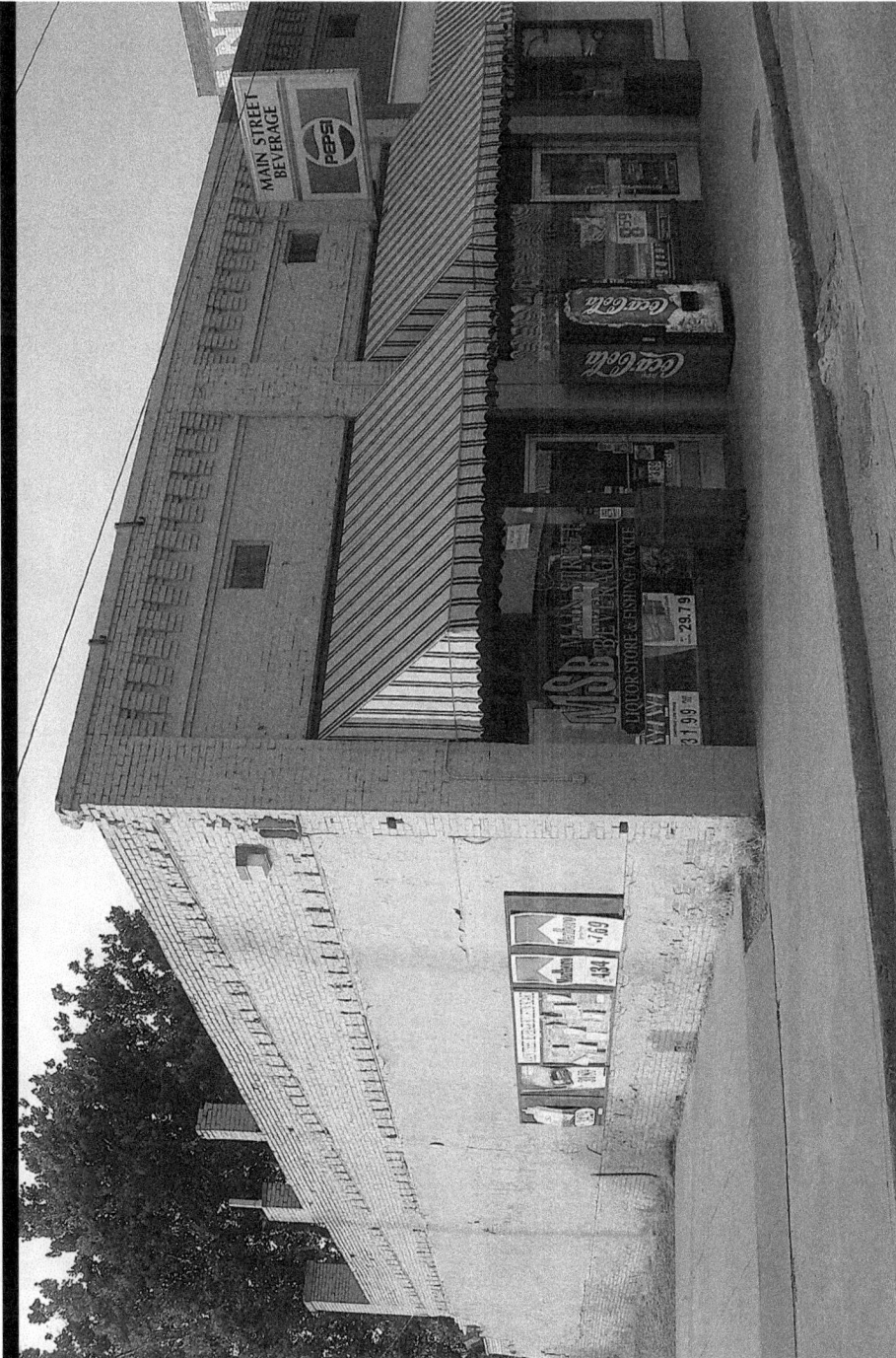

Brick storefronts on Emmett's Main Street recall the heyday of the Valley of Plenty. From 1920 to 1939, after fire destroyed the courthouse, the building held the assessor's office.

Jimmy Emerson/Flickr

The Crescent Rim development sparked controversy. In a neighborhood of single-family homes, protesters said the upscale condo project was "too dense."

Does dense make
• •
SENSE?

by Cindy Gould

oise's leaders have long favored infill—new development on vacant or underutilized land within existing developed areas—as a means to revitalize neighborhoods and prevent sprawl. But one person's infill can spark another's outrage, as a recent residential condominium project on Boise's Bench amply illustrates. During 2004-05, Clark Development's project on Crescent Rim Drive became a frequent news item as it worked its way through a series of public meetings en route to its eventual approval. As many as 300 residents in the Depot Bench neighborhood expressed their opposition in letters to the editor and at Planning and Zoning Commission and City Council hearings. One of the neighbors, Megan Montage, summed up the heightened interest at the time in the *Boise Weekly*: "Developers are watching because they're seeing how much push-room they have; neighbors are watching this to see how much the city will protect their neighborhoods."

At the center of the infill debate was Crescent Rim developer Bill Clark. An advocate of mixed-use, transit-friendly development, Clark's downtown projects include the Veltex Building and Jefferson Place. As a project manager, his credits include Hidden Springs and the Eagle River commercial-residential park. Clark, who is on the board of Idaho Smart Growth, said he tends to have a niche in more hard-to-do projects and knew he would have opposition. "Infill projects are not like building on the fringe where there are no neighbors; when you have neighbors there is frequently opposition. You are going into an existing context, surrounded by existing development and patterns that have been there for a long time ... and you are changing that. There is general resistance to change in a neighborhood environment," Clark explained.

Clark's property on Crescent Rim sits west of the Boise Depot between Peasley Street and Kipling Road. It is part of the Depot Bench neighborhood, one of the most diverse in Boise. The neighborhood boasts the Ahavath Beth Israel Synagogue and its community garden for refugees and Vista Village, the oldest shopping center in Boise. In a 2004 report, city planners stated the Central Bench, which includes the Depot Bench neighborhood, was a first-tier suburb, meaning it was threatened by disinvestment. City officials were—and still are—concerned that the oldest areas surrounding the downtown core are likely to have private abandonment and disinvestment as growth moves outward. In other cities a downward spiral begins as these neighborhoods become increasingly unattractive and dangerous. Boise, for the most part, has not had this problem, but city officials believe it is important to react to early warning signs of disinvestment.

Infill, a concept that has been in Boise's Comprehensive Plan since 1997, is one way to revitalize those areas. "It has long been a policy to encourage redevelopment of existing places that have become disinvested or of land that has been skipped over as the city developed," explained council member Elaine Clegg. Much of the land slated for the Crescent Rim project was vacant after an old bakery on the site was torn down. In the Planning Division's 2004 report, city planners welcomed Crescent Rim, stating, "The proposed project will constitute a significant private investment on property that has been vacant and the subject of code enforcement efforts for a number of years. The quality of this project will promote additional interest and private investment in the area, thus combating the trend of disinvestment that the City has documented in the area."

Clark saw the location's potential for a high-quality development and he was determined to design the condominiums in a way that took advantage of the view and was compatible with the neighborhood. "The site is in a very well-established and high-quality neighborhood. We spent quite a bit of time deciding on an appropriate design, one that would fit the neighborhood. Because it is a high-priced neighborhood, we thought that it could contain a luxury, larger-in-size condominium-type development ... one that is

City of Boise

View of the partially completed development from Crescent Rim Drive. The development was reduced in height and limited to 79 residential units.

in close proximity to the downtown core, which is in agreement with the goals of reduced traffic and sprawl. I started talking to the neighborhood before I had an architect, but there was opposition from the very beginning," Clark said. Residents expressed several concerns about the development's impact on the neighborhood—too high, too dense and too much additional traffic. And they were hopping mad about the removal of 13 trees from the property early in the process.

The Planning and Zoning Commission held the first of three hearings on Clark's Crescent Rim development on December 13, 2004, and the spark of opposition became a firestorm. So many people wished to testify at the

Idaho Statesman

Developer Bill Clark standing over a model of the Crescent Rim development. The buildings were meant to revitalize the Bench neighborhood.

hearing that the commissioners extended it to their next meeting on January 10, 2005. At issue was a conditional-use permit, which allows the city to consider special uses that are not a matter of right by zoning codes but may be desirable for a particular area. It enables the city to control certain uses that could have a detrimental effect on the community. And it allows the commission to determine how compatible a design is with the neighborhood and the impacts the project may have. The decision to grant or deny a conditional-use permit is made after a public hearing process.

Although city planners identified the area south of the development as tier one and at risk of disinvestment, the area most affected by the project was not tier one. The homes along Crescent Rim east and west of the development are in a traditional, well-maintained neighborhood composed mostly of one- and two-story houses. The land that Clark Development purchased included three types of zoned uses: R-1C (single family) on the southwest and east sides, R-3D (multi-family) in the center and a small area of A-1 (open space). The city's Planning Division staff report for Clark Development's original conditional-use permit stated that the project was consistent with the Depot Bench Neighborhood Plan completed in 2002. That plan, approved by the neighborhood association and city, zoned 62 percent of the property as multi-family and recognized the property as a potential site for infill of up to 157 dwelling units. In September 2004, Clark applied for a conditional-use permit that would allow him to distribute the density across the zoning lines on the property, which would allow more density in areas zoned for single-family housing. "We applied to have the dominant zone (multi-family) applied to all the property," said Clark, who also asked for a building height that exceeded the dimensional standard for the area. The proposal also entailed removal of an existing apartment building and three homes. During the December 13 hearing on the use permit, city planner Karen Gallagher explained that the proposed development was well within density limits, with the developer asking for almost 10 fewer dwelling units per acre than the zoning allowed.

The opposition made itself heard at the December 13 hearing. Neighborhood representative Jack Cortabitarte said, "The neighborhood preservation committee and the Depot Bench Neighborhood Association have never said 'no development' in the eight months we've been assessing this issue with the developer. Quite the contrary and he [Clark] knows that. In fact from day one the neighborhood told Mr. Clark that we want it to fit, we want it to transition properly with the existing neighborhood in height and bulk to complement the existing character and historical nature of our area. The neighborhood was ready to accept the project if it fit." In an effort to resolve some of the issues the city initiated a mediation session, which both the neighborhood association and the developer agreed to in late 2004, but the meeting failed to produce an agreement. Objections to the height and mass of the development dominated most of the testimony at the December hearing. The proposal was to build four buildings that stepped up in height from two to three stories along Kipling Road and Peasley Street, with four stories in the middle of the development. Cortabitarte testified: "The project overwhelmed the single-story homes that surrounded it and was incompatible with the surrounding architecture and character of the neighborhood." He added that issuing a height variance to allow four-story buildings to reach a total of 62-plus feet was not consistent with city code, which states, "Building and site design shall provide for a transition into the surrounding neighborhood to insure compatibility." The neighbors felt the proper transition was one, two and three stories only. Clark told the commission that by taking away the height of the buildings he lost maybe 10-12 highly desirable units. "I don't yet know the full implications of it; that's why I say these conditions are not really workable because we started with a density reduction from the very beginning trying to keep this site open," he said. Clark added during the hearing that he thought by reducing the heights on Peasley and Kipling he could add another story in the middle of the project, a concept that was suggested by area neighbors.

Neighbors also expressed concern about the increased traffic on the narrow streets that surround the development. Prior to the hearing Clark Development initiated a traffic study investigating the proposed project's effect on traffic. The study was presented to the Ada County Highway District and approved. However, the highway district acknowledged the 98-unit project would push surrounding street volumes close to their maximum capacity of 2,000 trips by generating 459 additional vehicle trips per day. Several people disagreed with the traffic study. During the January 2005 hearing Megan Montage, who helped write the traffic study for the 2002 Depot Bench Neighborhood Plan, said the study underestimated the additional vehicles, which could range from 582 to 631, depending on what methods were used to count them. But Planning and Zoning accepted the highway district opinion that the development wouldn't push traffic volumes over accepted standards. Some also voiced concerns related to the stability of the subsurface conditions along the Bench and water saturation from the nearby canal. They were concerned that the slope would not support the additional weight and the runoff from the development. During the December 13 hearing both the developer and the neighborhood brought experts to testify about the geological issue. If water came from the canal and flowed beneath the proposed site, people claimed, the sheer weight of the Crescent Rim project was likely to impact stability along the bench. Diane Myklegard, representing the Parkview East condominiums set into the slope across Crescent Rim Drive, told the commissioners that the condominium association had worked to stabilize the hill over the past 20 years and they were very concerned. Clark Development later installed a drainage system that reduces the amount of groundwater that flows toward the Parkview East condominiums by collecting the water and releasing it at a slower rate.

On January 24, 2005, the commission issued a denial of the plans as submitted. The "*Idaho Statesman*" quoted Commissioner Gene Fadness: "We liked the condo project because it could help revitalize the neighborhood through infill, but there are concerns about heights and setbacks from the street. We think he [Clark] is very close." In the same *Statesman* article

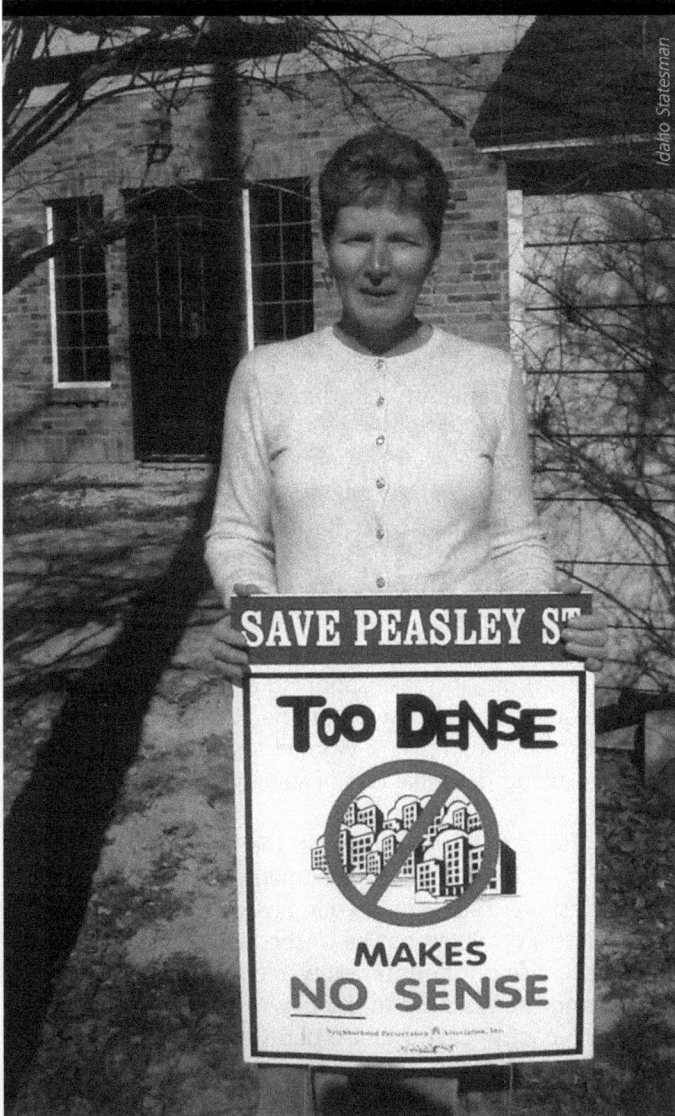

Moira Elcox in the Depot Bench Neighborhood placed a sign criticizing the Crescent Rim development.

Depot Neighborhood Association president Russ Thompson said, "It still creates a large mass on that corner. He still has a ways to go." On May 4, 2005, Clark Development returned to Planning and Zoning with a modified plan that reduced the number of units from 98 to 86. The units were set back from the street and the height in the center was reduced from five stories to four. City planning director Hal Simmons determined that the revised application, with a transitional third story along Kipling and Peasley, mitigated the neighbors' concerns about height and mass, even though height exceptions were still needed in parts of the development. Planners felt that because it was not one large building, but rather broken into four buildings with space between, the revised plan reduced the mass and would be more appealing to the neighborhood.

The *Idaho Statesman* reported that more than 150 people turned out for the May 4 hearing on Clark's revised plan. Some were wearing "Too dense makes no sense" badges and some carried signs outside City Hall to protest the development. Clark testified that the reduction of units was "very painful" in terms of the financial consequences for the project. He reiterated that under the zoning laws a much larger development was possible. Cortabitarte told the commission the neighborhood felt the change was a very good start, but the development was still too big and didn't fit. He presented a computerized model of the project with the neighboring houses. He put the perspective at eye level from Peasley, Kipling and Alpine and asked the commissioners if they felt the transition was reasonable. John Gannon of the neighborhood association testified that the Depot Bench Neighborhood Plan did not support high density along Peasley and Kipling, and that they were zoned R-1C to provide a buffer for more density in the middle of the property. "The neighbors are entitled to rely on that characteristic," he said. Chris Blanchard, who lives in the area south of the development, spoke in support of the development: "It will increase the property taxes for local schools, increase the property values in the immediate area, help the neighborhood get a bus route, increase shopping at Vista Village and bring revitalization to this area," he said. However, the "Crescent Rim Group," as Russ Thompson described them, were worried about the quality of the development and the resulting potential loss of value to their homes if it was done poorly.

At the May 4 meeting, after a 6 1/2-hour hearing, the Planning and Zoning Commission unanimously approved the development, while acknowledging the opposition. Commissioner Fadness stated in his comments, "The zoning allowed many more units, but would not be of the quality of this type." To him this was a compromise on the total allowable and what was best for the city. He felt that since it was close to the downtown area, people would walk, reducing the impact of cars. He also believed that because of its proximity to the Depot, eventually there would be proximity to urban transit. Commissioner Brandy Wilson expressed her remorse that a compromise between the developer and the neighborhood was not reached. But she too said, "We have to look at the big picture ... if they are to preserve farmland and the Foothills, reduce car miles and accommodate growth, people would have to expect infill development."

Larry Burke

Built in 1926, the Peasley House echoes the California Mission Revival of the 1925 Boise Depot. Critics fear that the nearby development would compromise the historic streetscape of single-family homes.

The neighborhood appealed the approval to the City Council. The hearing on August 31, 2005, drew a crowd of 170 people, lasted until after midnight and resumed the next evening, again running past midnight. At 2 a.m. on September 1, the City Council voted 3-1 to approve the project, but with some conditions of their own. The council reduced the number of units from 86 to 79 because they felt that there would be adverse impacts on traffic. To reduce the mass, the City Council required an open pedestrian passage to break the buildings along Kipling and Peasley. To make the project more compatible and transition better with existing houses they eliminated the fourth floors on the two buildings along Kipling and Peasley. Clark also agreed to provide $100,000 toward neighborhood improvements, including signage, landscaping and some traffic controls. The bulk of that money will be paid once the tenth unit has sold.

Construction on phase I began in late 2006, but the project stalled in 2008 when the real estate market deteriorated. To date, the exteriors of the

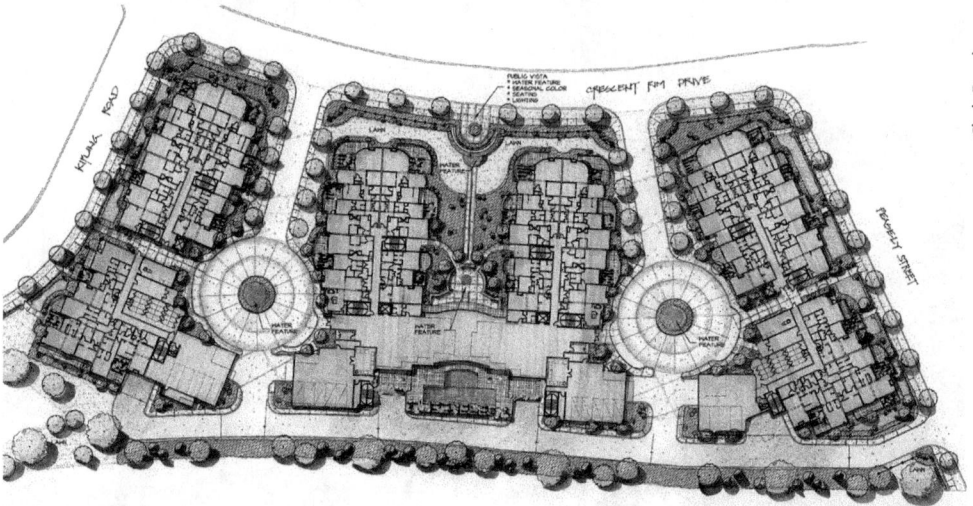

Clark Development's plan for the Crescent Rim project shows four buildings.
The housing crash of 2008 delayed condo construction. Exterior work
on two of the four buildings is now complete.

two center buildings have been completed, along with underground parking
garages for all four buildings, some landscaping and interior work on three
of the units. Clark Development is ready to resume work on landscaping and
on the interior of the remaining 38 unfinished units. "We have 6-7 months
of work ... then we plan to begin marketing again," said Clark. Construction
of the two buildings along Peasley and Kipling must wait until after the real
estate market improves. "We'll see how quickly the market absorbs the units
we have already built," said Clark. Turf covers the foundations of the two
buildings to preserve them for future use and to lessen the impact of open
construction on the neighborhood. Those buildings include 38 of the total
79 units, which average 2,000 square feet each. Clark estimates that the first
phase has cost $30 million.

The yearlong tussle over the Crescent Rim project left the neighborhood and city in agreement that they needed to improve the planning
process for infill projects. In his 2005 State of the City address Mayor David
Bieter said, "The controversy over the project highlighted the need for
change; we need a better process in fairness to everyone." Both the city and

the neighborhood acknowledged that infill is desirable, and by working together they can plan on future growth that protects the unique character of the neighborhood and supports development that is compatible. Boise is currently updating its comprehensive plan, called *Blueprint Boise*. The Depot Bench Neighborhood updated its plan in 2007. One goal is to help increase the level of predictability for residents about the potential for future changes in their areas and to inform the development community about areas where future development is desirable. Idaho Smart Growth has published two recent studies on infill in Boise. The latest, released in January 2010, develops policy recommendations to promote quality infill. "Basically, the recommendations place the onus on government to make sure its regulations are in order to support quality infill and the onus on the developers to be good neighbors," said council member Clegg, who wrote the report.

A Specific Area Plan, a process that brings developers, neighborhoods and the city staff together early in the planning stages, is one tool that has been added since Crescent Rim. "If you can meet with neighbors and bring back their concerns, then that helps. All parties get together to decide on the ground rules. Once those regulations are understood, there is no need to micromanage the project or load up the process with lots of hearings ... we take more time on the front end, but at the back end it is better for the development and the neighborhood," said Clegg. The city will remain a strong advocate of infill, but the challenge remains how to add new developments in existing neighborhoods without agitating the residents. Cooperation is the key, said Clegg. "Developers shouldn't make assumptions about what the neighbors want; the neighborhood shouldn't assume it will be a bad project, but rather learn about the development and make constructive comments; and the city has to ensure that all conversations will be three-way conversations."

• • •

Cindy Gould moved to Boise in 2003 to pursue her dream of getting a college education. She graduated in 2010 from Boise State University with a BBA cum laude in accountancy. She currently works in the City of Boise's Department of Finance and Administration.

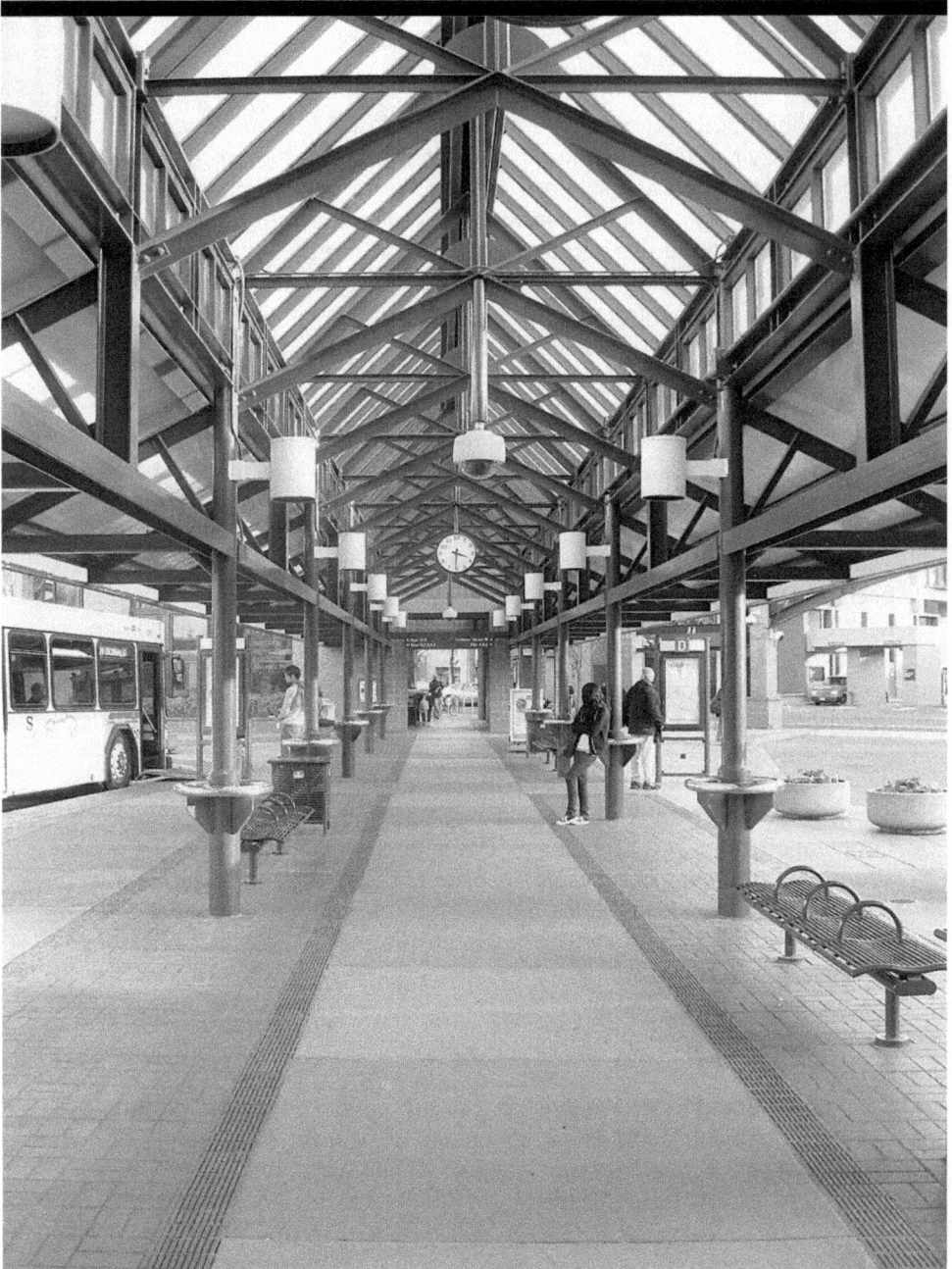

Streetcar Press

Eugene's Rosa Parks Plaza combines bus shelters, shopping, public art and a city library. Renamed for the civil rights pioneer in 2009, the plaza has been cited as a possible model for the proposed multimodal transit center in Boise's downtown.

Moving
TARGET

by Jennifer Otto

Some of the region's transportation needs, such as light rail and a high-capacity corridor, may be years away, but another key project is near the end of a long political and procedural journey—a downtown center that will serve as a hub for various transit services. Funding is already in place; the next step is to decide which location best suits transit needs and meets the litmus test of neighborhood acceptance. Called a multimodal center, transportation planners said it will enable the region's transit system to function more efficiently. Operated by Valley Regional Transit, the center will consolidate local and regional transit services in one location, serving as a hub for buses, vans, car pools and taxis. Bus rapid transit, streetcar and light-rail systems can be added as they develop.

The center will serve as a transfer or exit station for patrons using public transportation to reach Boise's downtown. Once at the multimodal center, they will be within walking or cycling distance of their destinations or can easily transfer to connecting bus routes or other modes of transportation.

The building will offer other services such as transit information, bike racks and commercial/public space. It will also serve as a storage area for various transit vehicles. The estimated cost of the center is $11 million. Valley Regional Transit received a Federal Transit Administration grant of $9.2 mil-

Streetcar Press

A well-designed transit center can contribute to urban renewal with city buses, regional bus rapid transit, light rail, streetcars, taxis, bike lockers and commuter vans. Pictured: bus-friendly municipal library at Eugene's Rosa Parks Plaza.

lion and the City of Boise and the Capital City Development Corporation provided the required 20 percent match for the federal funding.

One of the pivotal—and most controversial—decisions is the center's location. A site-selection committee composed of representatives from transportation agencies, planning organizations and local governments carefully examined five sites, including the current transit mall on the one-way streets of Main and Idaho. Between fall 2007 and spring 2009, the committee solicited public comments from business owners and citizens during three open houses, various downtown business meetings and newsletters. The site selection committee is now considering two potential locations. "Both are viable ... both will work equally well," said Rhonda Jalbert, who is overseeing the multimodal center project as Valley Regional Transit's capital infrastructure project manager. One, designated Site H, is along 11th Street between Bannock and Idaho streets, west of the Empire Building. The other, Site D, is along 12th Street between Idaho and Main streets, west of the Record Exchange. Both locations fit the criteria determined by the selection committee—they are downtown and within walking distance to many destinations, while also on existing bus routes and along a proposed downtown circulator route.

The selection committee preferred the 11th and Bannock location (Site H), but that choice drew strong opposition from neighbors, in particular the real estate development firm of Rafanelli & Nahas, which plans to construct a $100 million complex that includes a hotel, condominiums, office buildings, a park and plaza on land it owns across Bannock Street. In its May 6, 2010 issue, the *Idaho Statesman* reported that Rafanelli & Nahas, owner of the Boise Plaza, threatened to halt its own development plans for the nearby land. Citing security concerns, the developers wrote in an e-mail to city officials that they will "continue to oppose (the site) with all our efforts, influence and resources."

In December 2010, the City of Boise identified the 12th and Idaho property (Site D) as another location to consider. That site was one of the originals under consideration, but the property owner at the time was not interested in selling. But that has changed, and now both sites are under consideration. City spokesman Adam Park told the *Idaho Statesman* on December 14, 2010, "The alternative site may offer greater economic development benefits because of its potential for transit-oriented development to be built in coordination with the center itself." Rafanelli & Nahas project manager Scott Schoenherr also told the *Statesman* that the site was "less problematic for us."

There are a number of steps to be taken before construction begins. An environment assessment on Site H was completed and accepted by the Federal Transit Administration in June of 2009. A similar assessment is now underway for Site D; much of the material from the original study remains relevant and will help inform the new document. Jalbert says the new environmental assessment could add an additional six months to the selection process. Valley Regional Transit will conduct an open house to inform the public about the plans for Site D. Once the site selection is made, the

property will be appraised to determine the fair market value and land acquisition requirements. The appraisal and eventual contract must be submitted
to the Federal Transit Administration for approval. After the agency approves
the appraisal, the entitlement process will begin, which includes additional
environmental, site grading, building elevation and utility studies along with
the required application for a conditional use permit from Boise's Planning
and Zoning Commission. Once the entitlement process is completed the
design phase can begin, which is projected to take at least six months. The
construction design plans need city approval and building permits must be
issued before the project can finally move into the construction phase.
While no official construction groundbreaking date has been determined,
Jalbert says that Valley Regional Transit would like to start construction one
year after the site has been selected, which could be in the early spring of
2012. The actual construction of the multimodal center is projected to take
one year.

     Regardless of which site is selected, the City of Boise ultimately will be
a major player in the decision, even though Valley Regional Transit, in con-
junction with other planning agencies, is responsible for planning, funding
and building the center. Boise's Design Review Committee must ultimately
approve the site design and the Planning and Zoning Commission will issue
the conditional-use permit. Both of those steps require a public hearing
process in which an appeal by a private business or individual can be filed. It
already has been a long and involved process since the funds were approved
in 2005. While the money is not currently in jeopardy, Jalbert said it "is
expected that there is forward movement and that the grantee does not just
sit on the funds."

     Selection committee members have conducted visits to other transit
centers to glean ideas, but Kathleen Lacey, a comprehensive planner with
the City of Boise, explained that the actual design depends on the final building site purchased, community needs and available funds. Once those are
determined, Zimmer, Gunsul and Frasca, the architectural design firm from
Portland that won the bid, will complete the design. Multimodal centers,
said Lacey, don't have to be monolithic concrete structures that distract from
the surrounding area, as evidenced by the award-winning centers in
Charlotte, North Carolina, Boulder, Colorado or Bellevue, Washington. A well-
planned and constructed multimodal center can include a variety of functions. Jalbert said the proposed plans for Boise call for a two-story structure,
with the ground floor holding the transit ticket office, a public lobby, a bus
operators' lounge, a passenger plaza and sheltered waiting areas, 12 bus
bays, public restrooms, a visitor center, transit information kiosks, bicycle

Larry Burke

Boise State University has won a COMPASS award for promoting mass-transit alternatives to the automobile. A new transit center in the Student Union has a waiting lounge with a live GPS feed on shuttle buses.

storage, vanpool and carpool drop-off/pick-up areas, a taxi stand, retail development and a police substation. The second level could be for public parking to replace the current spaces lost in development of the site.

How important is the multimodal center to the overall transportation picture in Treasure Valley? Lacey pointed out that building the center as a first step is important since it will be a major component in the region's long-range plan. She explained that a central hub improves patron services and the transit system because buses and other transportation modes can arrive and depart from one location, which in turn offers riders more options for easier transfer to other transportation. A long delay in the construction of the multimodal center could affect the other phases of the regional transportation plan—a downtown circulator and a high-capacity corridor—that will move the valley closer to meeting the goal of reducing traffic congestion and improving air quality, Lacey added.

A mass public transit system in Boise is a long-term project, but transportation systems in other cities can help gauge the need for one in Boise. In

Architecture Things

Fabric cones recycle rainwater from the roof of the $22 million Rosa Parks Transit Center in the heart of downtown Detroit. Boiseans have cited Detroit as an innovate example of bus-shelter architecture.

the 1970s, Portland was much like Boise is now—a growing city in beautiful surroundings with a population of about 380,000 and a county population of more than 550,000. With an eye on the growth potential of not only the city but also its many suburbs, three counties formed the TriMet transportation district that now consists of high-speed light rail, buses and streetcars that serve the region. The Portland Streetcar, opened in 2001, has successfully helped revitalize areas of the city that had fallen into disrepair. Now places like the Pearl District, Brewery Blocks and the River District are destination spots with restaurants, small businesses and mixed-use housing for people of different income, job types and cultures.

If the past is prologue, Boise will be facing even more growth in the next 25 years. According to the data gathered for 2006 Communities in Motion, a regional long-range transportation plan, the valley currently holds 42 percent of the state's population, with a total of 504,000 residents and a projected growth to more than 1 million by 2035. People and jobs most likely will be spread out over a multi-county region, which means planners are looking for ways to move the increased numbers of people. In 2007, planners initiated the Treasure Valley High Capacity Transit Study to deal with the projected traffic and growth. The valley-wide mobility plan included all forms of current transit services, such as ValleyRide bus services and Commuteride, in addition to future projects such as Bus Rapid Transit or light rail. The study concluded that three related projects were essential for the valley's transportation future: a multimodal transportation center, a downtown Boise circulator and a high-capacity corridor. These three projects are to be phased in over time

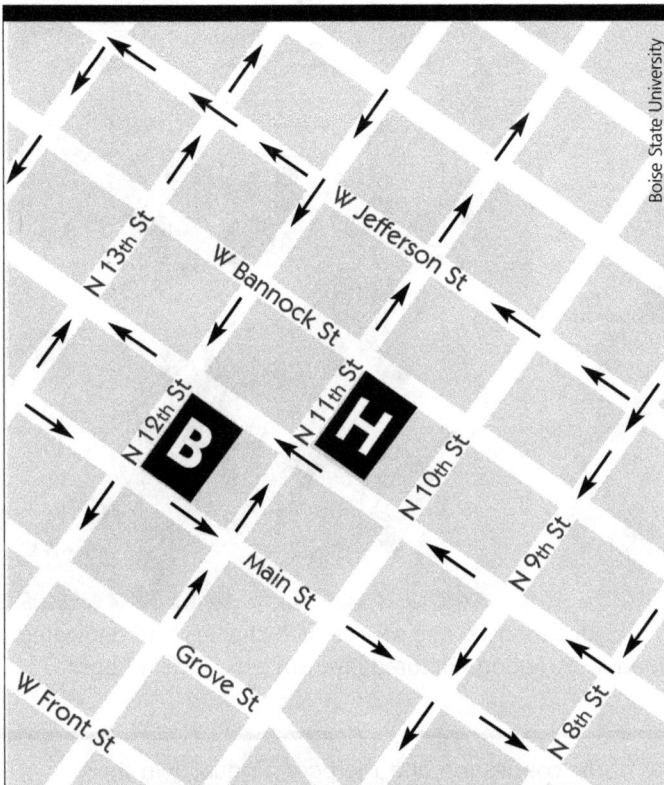

Possible locations of Boise's multimodal center include Site H (11th at Bannock) and Site B (12th at Main).

World Resources Institute

Bus rapid transit, or BRT, provides trainlike bus service with shelters and dedicated lanes for long-range regional commuting. Pictured: Transmilenio BRT in Bogotá, Columbia.

to help solve both the traffic congestion and the poor air quality in the valley.

The Boise region already has some basic-level transit centers in place but none offers the myriad of services planned for the downtown Boise multimodal center. For example, a center located in the Boise Towne Square Mall parking lot consists of just two covered shelters and bus lanes. Jalbert notes that one of Valley Regional Transit's goals is that as the population increases there will be more types of these small transit centers to serve as hubs throughout Ada and Canyon counties, but none would be as complex or visible as the multimodal center.

Boise State University just opened its own transit center, funded with a Federal Transportation Administration grant and 20 percent matching from the Student Union and Transportation Services. Built on the west entrance of the Student Union, Smart Growth and the promotion of alternative types of transportation are at the forefront of this project, said Casey Jones, director of transportation and parking services. While Boise State's transit center is a completely separate project from the downtown Boise multimodal center, it operates on the same concept—consolidating transit information and services; carpool/vanpool, regional bus and Bronco Shuttle stops; an indoor lobby and waiting lounge; and bicycle parking all at one common location. The current Boise Bronco Shuttles are already outfitted with GPS units and students can utilize a website with a live feed to locate each shuttle and the expected arrival time for each of the 19 stops. The website can be accessed by computer or cell phone and in the new transit center lobby. Valley Regional Transit is working toward having many of the same capabilities for their buses in the future.

Mass transportation can be part of the answer to the complex problem of limited resources, sprawl and individual needs. The Boise Valley has grown to a size where the need to look at mass transportation modes is becoming critical. For many, the benefits of a public mass transportation system in the valley far outweigh the costs. Let us hope that in the coming decades, we look back at the multimodal center as just one footstep in the beginning phase of a larger transit project that changed the course of history in the valley.

• • •

Jennifer Otto is a senior sociology major attending Boise State University part time. She holds a full-time job working with non-profit, faith-based and federally-funded agencies that provide services to the homeless across the state.

City of Boise

The League of American Bicyclists includes Ada County on its list of 150 bike-friendly communities.

Biking
BOISE
by Marc Orton

Wilderness crusader John Muir claimed he wasn't blindly opposed to progress. Rather, he was opposed to blind progress. Likewise, Treasure Valley residents are taking Muir's words to heart by responding to urban sprawl with a time-tested technology—the bicycle. This two-wheeled revolution has lead to some eye-opening numbers. According to recent Ada County Highway District estimates, during warm weather months Ada County residents take as many as 55,000 bicycle trips per day, thus eliminating 37,000 miles of daily vehicle travel and reducing emissions by almost 60 tons each day. Impacts like those are certainly incentives to encourage more bicycle use, which is one reason why the highway district has drafted an extensive plan to improve the cycling environment throughout the county and its six cities. The Roadways to Bikeways Plan, approved in 2009, is a comprehensive study of the county's cycling infrastructure, with a long list of strategies to expand the on-street bikeway network, connect gaps, address constrained areas and promote alternative

Sears & Roebuck

In 1896 an alarmed Boise city council passed speed limits for biking. On boardwalks, within 40 feet of pedestrians, the maximum speed was four-miles per hour. Pictured: Sear's catalogue illustration, about 1914.

transportation in the Treasure Valley over the next 50 years. The plan also provides detailed analysis of the cycling environment in each Ada County city and makes specific recommendations for improvements.

"Years ago we used to spend all of our money on roads," said highway district commissioner John Franden. "There was an attitude in the community of 'Why in the world would you spend money on bike lanes?' There was no overarching plan in the past ... biking is a big part of the equation now." The intent is to eventually create an interconnected bicycle network to make commuting in the Treasure Valley more accessible through new bicycle routes, park and ride areas, bus systems and bicycle facilities. The plan offers recommendations to update the system of bike lanes and shared roadways.

According to the highway district plan, 95 percent of all the county residents will be within a quarter mile of a bike lane or route.

With one of the most extensive and celebrated Greenbelts in the country, a mountain bike trail system that is the envy of every urban area and a bona fide Olympic cycling champion in residence, the region's reputation is growing. In 2004, Ada County was awarded bronze medal status as a Bicycle Friendly Community by the League of American Bicyclists. While the majority of cyclists ride for recreation, there is a sizable number who saddle up for the daily commute to work. The highway district estimated that 4,000 commuters use a bicycle as their primary mode of daily transportation. In a 2007 highway district survey of more than 1,200 riders, 62 percent said that commuting to work was the main reason they cycle. The current Roadways to Bikeways Plan builds on two previous efforts, both of which improved the cycling infrastructure. The 2005 Pedestrian Bicycle Transition Plan laid the groundwork for the current plan and the Ridge-to-Rivers Pathway Plan built a multi-use path and trail system between the Boise River and the Boise Foothills. In recent years, Ridge-to-Rivers has incorporated more than 130 miles of trails. Roadways to Bikeways will build on the foundations laid by those previous efforts.

Another key aspect of the plan is safety. Concerns about safety have historically been the single greatest reason people do not commute by bicycle, as indicated in Lou Harris polls as early as 1991. A Safe Routes to School survey in 2004 similarly found that 30 percent of parents consider traffic-related danger to be a barrier to allowing their children to walk or bike to school. The 2007 highway district survey indicates that one of the main reasons people don't cycle is a concern for safety. Half of those surveyed cited a lack of bike lanes and too many vehicles as key problems with the existing bicycle network. Addressing those concerns is a major objective of the highway district plan. One new program that includes a cycling component is Safe Routes to Schools, which spends $4 million annually to build sidewalks, improve intersections and make other improvements so children can walk or cycle more safely to school. "If a bike lane can be put in, we will do that. But many times sidewalks have to double as bike lanes," explained Franden.

Ada County and its six cities already have a number of vastly popular bikeways—the Boise River Greenbelt, Hill Road, the north/south connection of 15th Street, Warm Springs Avenue and areas on the Central Bench. And Boise State is well underway on a 15-year plan to eliminate automobile and pedestrian conflicts with cyclists and connect the university with the surrounding neighborhoods and downtown. The next step is to build a complete bikeway network that links a variety of destinations—employment,

Boise police use mountain bikes to patrol downtown, the parks and 22 miles of Greenbelt. Founded in 1989, the bicycle unit has a sergeant and five full-time riders. Pictured: patrolling on Fourth of July, 2009.

shopping, school and recreation. The addition of support facilities such as directional signage and secure bicycle parking will enhance the network and encourage more people to bicycle, according to the plan. Of course, no plan is of value unless it can be implemented. And in many cases that leads to money. There is no budget set aside to fund the plan from start to finish. But some aspects of the plan are in progress, such as wayfinding signs on Parkcenter Boulevard and Hill Road, and sidewalk and lane additions to portions of Roosevelt and Boise avenues. Some improvements, like bike lanes on existing or new roads, already are incorporated into the district's budget. Now, whenever a road is expanded or rebuilt, bike lanes are included. No major road is built without a bike lane on it, said Franden. "The cost is not

Ada County Sheriff/keiljohnson/Flickr

The environment for cyclists has improved since the highway district began adding bike lanes to new and widened roads. Pictured: Ada County bike safety campaign.

inconsequential." If you add a bike lane on each side of the road, that widens the road by 10 feet. Doing that for 3-4 miles adds up to a lot of land to purchase and a lot of additional construction."

An improved cycling environment is important to the citizens of Ada County because it will create a more multimodal transportation system that promotes bicycling as a practical alterative to driving, and thus relieve congested roadways, reduce dependence on non-renewable fuels and enhance air quality. The notion of interconnectivity and cycling-friendly policies is not a modern ideal, but one that dates back more than 100 years. In the

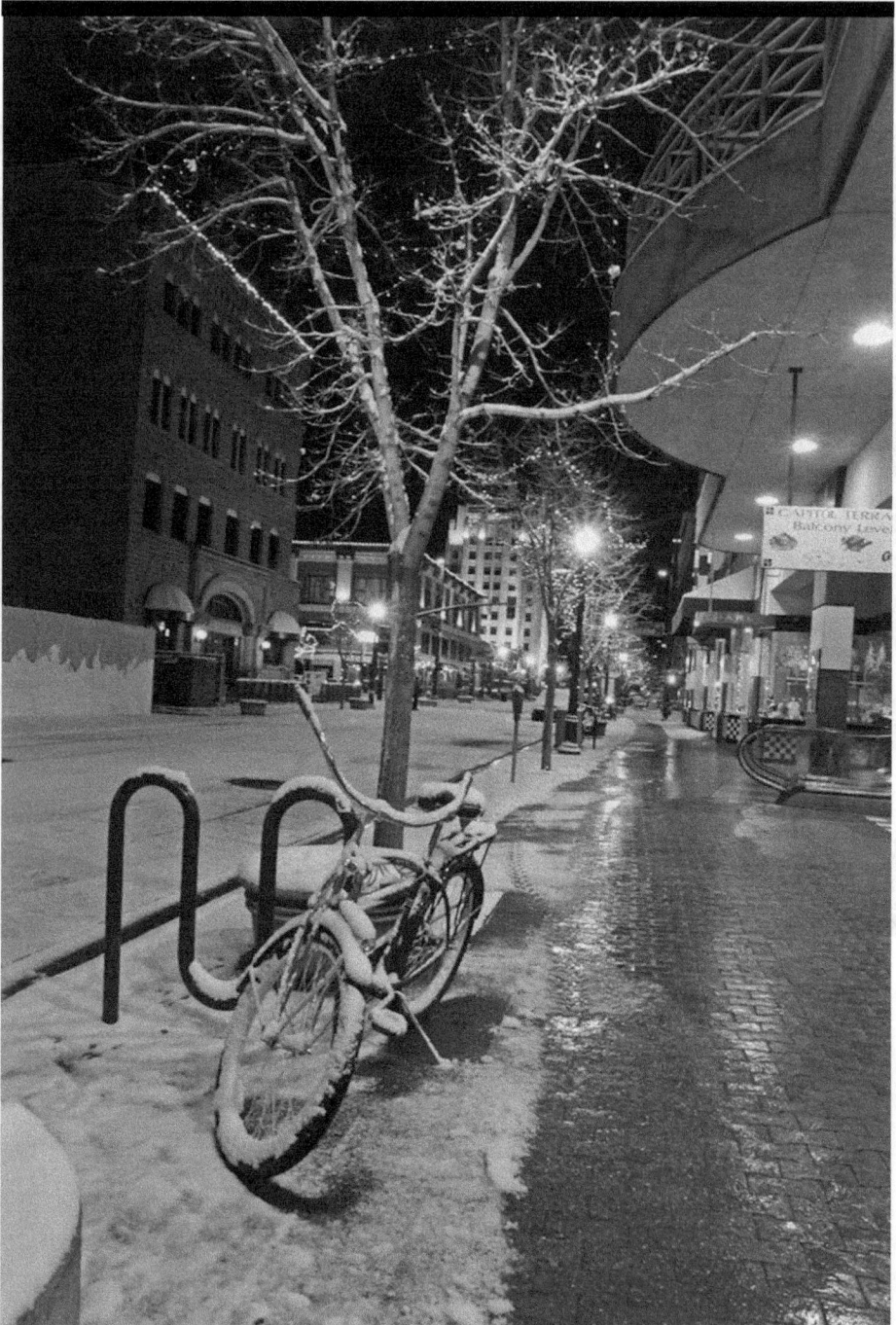

Eric Maier/Flickr

Cold riding grows in popularity as the price of gasoline soars. Boise bike commuters have been known to stud their own snow tires.

Treasure Valley, the beginning of the 20th century was an age of multimodal transportation. There were cycling clubs for bicycle enthusiasts, horse-drawn carriages, pedestrian accommodations and an Interurban trolley system. There was a range of transportation options in this era, a time in which the Treasure Valley was connected by its first form of mass transit—the trolley. However, the heyday of alternative transportation was short-lived. By the 1930s the rail lines were paved over and the automobile was affordable enough for people to welcome it with open arms. In the following decades, the Treasure Valley made way for the automobile, allowing suburban sprawl to push development further away from the town core and increasing citizens' reliance on the motor vehicle. All of this had little consequence until decades later when air quality reached the point where Ada County was close to "nonattainment" status in meeting federal air quality standards. Cycling may not be the answer to low air quality and urban sprawl, but it is an alternate mode of transit that can play an ever-increasing role in the valley's transportation picture. The bicycle is a low-cost and effective means of transportation that is non-polluting, energy-efficient, versatile, healthy and fun. Bicycling has been growing in popularity as many communities like Boise work to create more balanced transportation systems by giving cyclists a greater share of the roadway networks. Smart Growth ideals work seamlessly with cycling; it is transit-and pedestrian-oriented and encourages a greater mix of housing, commercial and retail uses. Cycling, and specifically the highway district plan, meshes well with those concepts, which are gaining more and more acceptance. "Improvements to the Boise cycling environment are driven by changes in the attitudes of the public ... more people today want to walk and ride bikes," said David Bartle, until recently chairman of the highway district's Bicycle Advisory Committee. "It is very clear now that the highway district has established an official policy to guide cycling infrastructure improvements and to identify key routes for investment. This reflects an attitude that has been evolving over the last 15 years ... to recognize it is increasingly important."

• • •

Marc Orton is completing his bachelor's degree in the applied science program with emphases in dispute resolution, communications and heavy equipment technology. He works for the Boise Bicycle Project and volunteers at the Village Bicycle Project.

M3 Companies

Spring Valley developers envision a 6,000-acre planned community with 7,000 homes in the foothills near Eagle.

Beyond

EAGLE

by Roman Lewis

Many towns in Idaho face the question of how to best manage growth. While some are successful in their bid to maintain a strong sense of community tied to their unique qualities, others suffer from a lack of cohesion in planning design and have lost their sense of culture and history, all of which contribute to a disjointed infrastructure and perpetuate aimless sprawl. The City of Eagle exemplifies the complex issues cities must confront in the face of the pressing demands of growth. The town is currently involved in a dynamic process with a developer whose properties' annexation will have far-reaching effects upon the future of the city and the surrounding area.

Population growth in Idaho has dramatically increased over the past decade. According to the U.S. Census, between 2000-09 Idaho witnessed a 19.5 percent increase in its total population, placing it fifth in the nation in overall percentage increase in population growth. Even with the recent economic downturn, Idaho still ranked 12th nationally in percentage

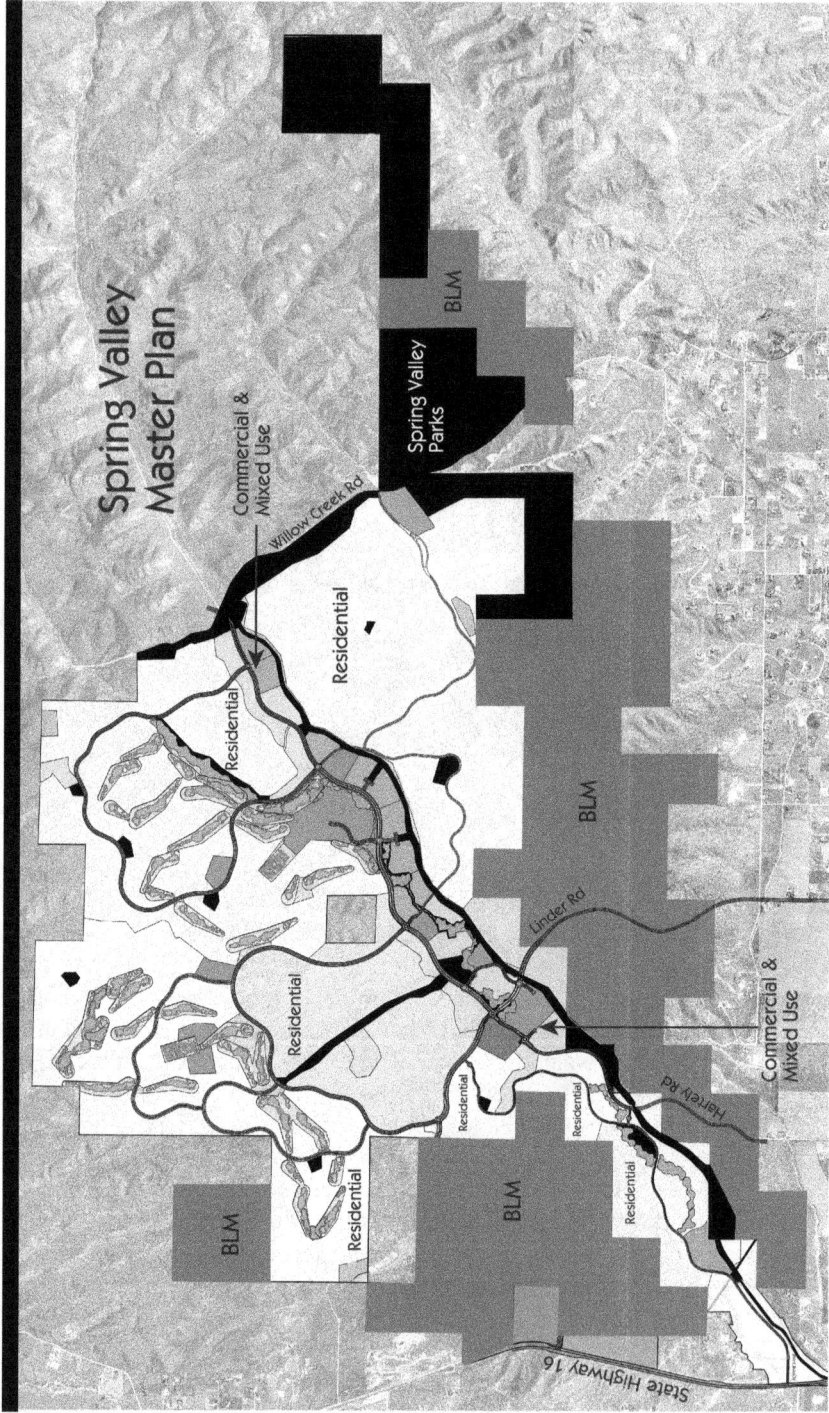

Spring Valley
Master Plan

Commercial &
Mixed Use

Willow Creek Rd

Residential

Residential

Spring Valley
Parks

BLM

Residential

BLM

Linder Rd

Residential

Commercial &
Mixed Use

Residential

Harrety Rd

Residential

BLM

BLM

Residential

State Highway 16

M3 Companies

The Spring Valley master plan features a mix of residential, commercial and recreational uses for the development east of Highway 16.

population growth in 2008-09. The Treasure Valley has borne the brunt of this substantial population boom, with Ada and Canyon counties ranking as the first and second most-populated areas in the state. Growth provides many benefits to a community. Besides the obvious expanded tax base, the diversity of population and business attracted to the community can greatly enhance the quality of life within the city and surrounding area. But challenges accompany the positive side of growth. Idaho's rapid population influx also has placed tremendous burdens on municipalities, leaving city leaders racing to develop strategies and forge consensus to mitigate the impact upon infrastructure and services. While cities possess a number of policy prescriptions, land use regulations and finance instruments to address the obstacles of growth, these options may not be systemically, financially or politically feasible, thus limiting the effectiveness of any response and creating a disconnect between the public's perception of their elected officials' competence and the constraints they must operate within.

Cities, developers and citizen groups face several key issues in responding to the growth. An examination of the background and issues surrounding M3 Eagle, recently named Spring Valley—a 6,000-acre planned community of more than 7,000 homes, shops, offices and amenities being developed by the M3 Companies in the foothills north of Eagle—could be instructive to other cities facing the dilemmas of growth. Numerous stakeholders are involved, foremost being the general public, but three others—the City of Eagle, M3 and the North Ada County Foothills Association—are central to the issues and can serve as proxies that address general themes that could arise in development projects all over the state. M3 Eagle is a case worth examining, for it is a development in progress, rich with instances of collaborative efforts among stakeholders as well as points of contention that have yet to be fully resolved. The general issues associated with this project illustrate the complexities of managing growth in Idaho.

Eagle is located 11 miles west of Boise in Ada County and is bordered by Boise and Garden City on the east and southeast respectively, Meridian on the south, Star to the west and unincorporated rangelands to the north. The city experienced a 61 percent population increase over a 9-year period (2000-09), as the city grew from 12,083 to 19,668. Strategically placed between the Boise River and the foothills, Eagle maintains a unique small town environment emphasizing its rural surroundings and traditional design. The city promotes the inherent natural beauty that enhances its quality of life and expends great effort to maintain numerous parks, water amenities and accessibility to walking, horse and bike paths. The surrounding landscape plays a lead role in Eagle's planning decisions and the city has created standards and design guidelines to maintain a balance between nature and development. Eagle's property tax levy rate is the lowest amongst its surrounding neighbors, with the next highest levy rate a little more than two times its own. Lower taxes combined with natural amenities are incentives for individuals looking for homes and business interests.

M3, a development company with headquarters in Arizona and an office in Eagle, determined that Eagle, with its reputation, size, demographics, locale and proximity to Boise, fit well with its development vision. In early 2005, M3 began purchasing sizeable tracts of private land in the foothills north of the city, properties that would become the foundation of the M3 Eagle planned development. As Gerry Robbins, M3 Eagle general manager, explained, "The company looks for reasonably priced land in areas that are in the path of future growth, have a sound basis for continued growth and vitality and have a location with high quality-of-life factors. Eagle met these criteria and we felt there was an opportunity to do something special here." Representatives from M3 met with then-Eagle Mayor Nancy Merrill to discuss the process for annexing their property, which was located in unincorporated Ada County, into the city and to devise a framework for negotiations on an agreement that would guide the development of the project. At the same time, the county was in the process of updating its comprehensive plan and drafting a future growth plan for the foothills, including the M3 property. This complicated matters for the city since the county intended to continue drafting its plan until credible evidence was presented showing that Eagle was in fact going to annex the land. Further, M3 Eagle's land was not contiguous to Eagle, so the company did not have a clear annexation path to the city. The Bureau of Land Management owned a chunk of land running along the property's southern edge, and other private lands blocked M3 Eagle's connection to the city. The public used the BLM land for a variety of outdoor recreational activities, and upon hearing that a development was proposed next to a cherished resource, community groups mobilized to demand representation in any decisions made over changes to the Eagle comprehensive plan that might favor development at the cost of environmental and public concerns.

During the initial planning phase, it was obvious that an open and honest dialogue was necessary to address the needs and concerns of all stakeholders. The City of Eagle was primarily concerned with the impacts that the development might have on the city if M3 Eagle remained as part of Ada County or for that matter, was annexed to its western neighbor Star. Mayor Merrill said that Eagle preferred that large developments near the city request annexation. "Development is going to occur, either on our outskirts (in Ada County) or in the city ... we would prefer that they be inside our city limits so that we can use our design standards and our comprehensive plan to make sure the developments fit in with Eagle's plan," Merrill told the *Idaho Statesman* in October 2006. Since M3 agreed, they needed to under-

Houses will be built in five "planning areas." The extent of the aquifer that will supply water to Spring Valley has been a source of contention between neighbors, developers and government agencies.

stand the city's requirements and processes. According to M3's Robbins, "The development has a 20-year build-out, so the sooner we could understand what was required by us (from the city) the quicker we could set about meeting those requirements." The community advocacy group most intimately involved in the process, the North Ada County Foothills Association, was primarily concerned with the effects that any development would have on the foothills area and the recreational opportunities and lifestyle enjoyed by the surrounding community. The foothills association's primary purpose was—and still is—to actively work with Ada County, the City of Eagle, water resource and transportation agencies, landowners and other

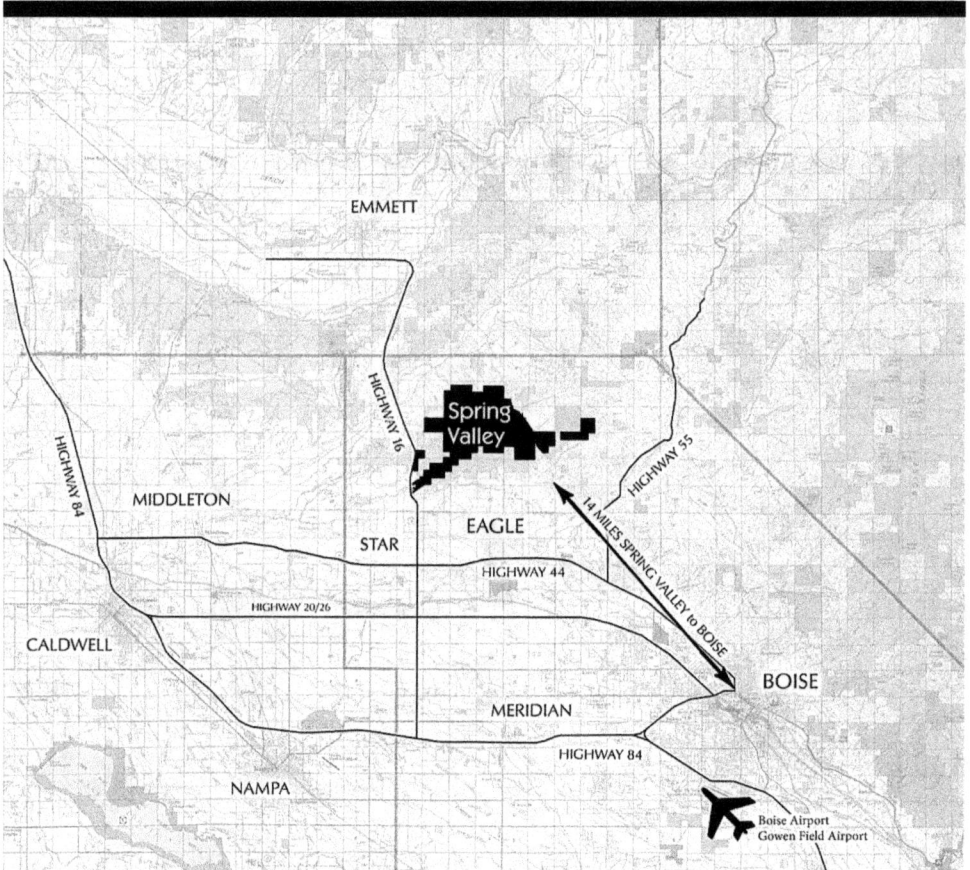

In 2009, when the City of Eagle annexed Spring Valley, M3 Companies advanced their development plan.

interested parties to create and implement a plan for the north Ada County foothills.

Because property rights have high priority and are well protected in Idaho, there are a limited number of regulations that developers must adhere to relative to other states. As former Eagle Mayor Phil Bandy put it, "The onus is really on the community in determining what should be required of the developer." This statement underscores the value of a well-defined comprehensive plan, for it determines what path the city will embark upon as it grows. Well-designed comprehensive plans enable cities to retain their character and unique culture, while vague plans may lead to a lack of cohesion with a city's overarching themes and values. Eagle needed to amend its comprehensive plan to include the proposed development, and this circumstance created the opportunity to expand its plan to encompass the entire north foothills area. The city formed committees consisting of developers, citizens, landowners and city staff to help prepare the proposed comprehensive plan amendments. This also created a mechanism for both the developer and leaders of advocacy groups to "sit at the table" together and work with the city.

A Pre-Annexation and Development Agreement is a legally binding contract between the city and developer that sets the terms and conditions of the project. This agreement, endorsed by M3 and Eagle in December 2007, became the blueprint for the project and locked in each party's obligations. Numerous studies, evaluations and testimony were taken, with public hearings playing a key role in providing citizens the opportunities to voice their opinions on a number of issues and challenge the assumptions of the developer and city. Some of the primary concerns presented at these meetings by those opposed to foothills development included: the potential damage to native wildlife and habitat; potential changes in status and trusteeship of the BLM land separating the development from the city; and the proposed plans for new roads and infrastructure to manage the eventual volume of traffic as well as wear and tear on pre-existing thoroughfares and infrastructure.

The foothills provide a natural habitat to a variety of plant and animal species native to the region. Concerns were raised about the effect of development and increased traffic on wildlife and habitat, as well what measures the developer was willing to take to mitigate damage. Concern over the plan to address slick spot peppergrass, a native foothills grass recently placed on the endangered species list, also emerged after a lightning strike in the foothills burned a number of houses along with the rare grass. Some questioned how the city would be able to handle a similar brushfire scenario, only this time with additional development. Some interest groups advocated that environmental factors should be the primary determinant in land utilization. They questioned how seriously the developer and city considered these environmental factors as features to be protected and maintained. The foothills association voiced concern over plans for the BLM land, as a proposed "land swap" between M3 and the BLM appeared to be an option that would address the issues surrounding annexation. This was a highly contentious issue, as a wide range of individuals and interest groups demanded a voice in any decision involving the transfer of longstanding public lands to a private party. Although M3 had stated that its goal was to develop and maintain the area as a system of public parks and open space, those opposed to the land swap did not agree in principle to any public/private transfer. This option was eventually dropped, but remains an important issue across the state. M3 did later purchase land contiguous to the city, thus meeting that annexation requirement.

Citizens of Eagle and the surrounding area also were concerned about the effects that a development of this scale would have on existing roadways and infrastructure, as well as the costs involved in building and maintaining a number of additional thoroughfares and infrastructure components that would be required to serve the potential users living in and around the development. A phrase commonly used was that "the developer must pay his fair share of the costs," and this included additional infrastructure and associated costs. Citizens were concerned that they would bear the true costs of the development and that the developer would not shoulder his fair share of the burden. These issues were only a few of those raised at the meetings, and they continue to be points of contention. However, three overarching strands —the total number of units in the development; their distribution within the property; and the potential economic and environmental impacts of the development—would eventually play a defining role in the city's calculus for determining the impact of the M3 Eagle annexation, and serve as the focal points of opposition to the project by the foothills association and other groups. These issues reflected many of the concerns held by all parties involved, and the eventual decision made by the city to annex the property hinged primarily on the ability to develop a workable framework to establish terms that met the interests of the City of Eagle, its citizens and the developers.

Developers planned for an initial maximum density of 12,010 units. Both the City of Eagle and the foothills association agreed that this number was too high, and did not fit within the context of the foothills and the rural/urban development environment the city was trying to maintain. This led to prolonged negotiations with the developer as each side debated the merits of the case. The final negotiated settlement was reached through compromise between the developer's desire for units and the city and citizens' desire for community amenities and open space. The city ultimately approved a base project density of 0.5 units per gross acre, or 3,003 dwelling units, and 245 acres for non-residential use. However, the city would allow additional units if the developer would build amenities such as a community center or reserve land for open space. Through the application of those provisions, the maximum density became 1.19 units per gross acre, or

7,153 dwelling units, and 245 acres for non-residential use. Residents and the foothills association consistently expressed concern over the potential for loss of open space, but the city created a plan that appealed to citizen concerns while providing incentives that would enable the developer to increase

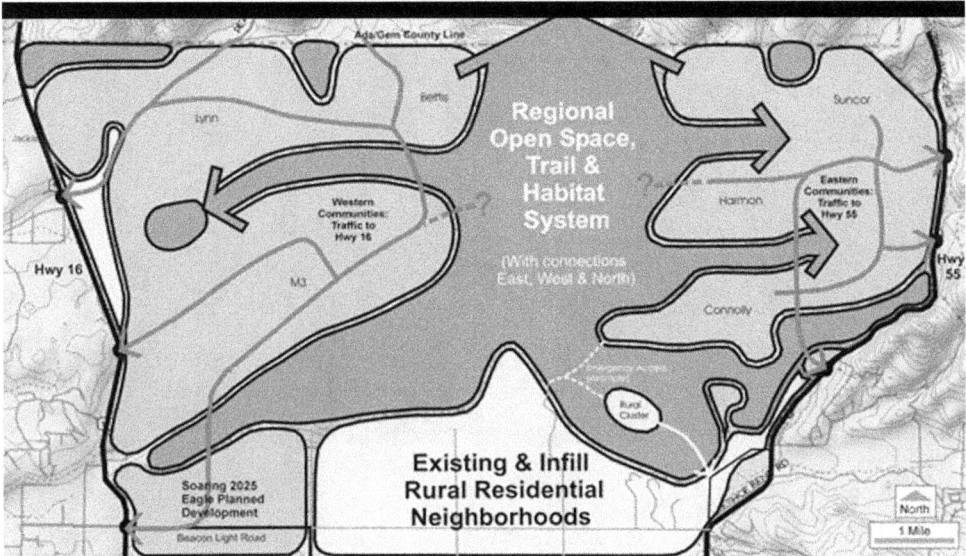

Developers promote Spring Valley as a mix of houses and open space that maintains the area's rural heritage.

the number of units allowed, satisfying the city's desire to manage growth. M3 found these conditions acceptable and began incorporating them into the design of the project.

The developer's intent in the overall design vision was to incorporate and emulate the natural topography to facilitate a complementary connection between the natural and man-made landscape. This vision also fit within the city's overall direction for hillside developments and addressed the foothills association's concerns in preserving the natural environment as well. Although each stakeholder's interpretation of what this meant and how it should be executed varied in scope, it provided the basis for the framework of the development plan. The M3 Eagle development is comprised of five different Planning Areas—Big Gulch, Northern Residential, Southern Residential, Southwestern Residential and Highway Mixed-Use/Business Park, all scheduled to be phased in over a 20-year period. Each Planning Area is defined by

Arden Tree Farms

Annually some 8,000 deer and 1,000 elk winter in the Boise Foothills. More than 200 are killed by cars. Pictured: mule deer, the dominate species near Boise.

a unique design based on its associated location and topography, existing and planned transportation corridors, mix of commercial and residential uses, land(s) set aside for public facilities and open space. M3 and the city agreed that open space was an intrinsic characteristic of the locale's identity and that open space would comprise a minimum of 20 percent of the development. (The city standard was 10 percent.) They also agreed that within all Planning Areas a minimum of 50 percent of all dwelling units, 65 percent of all single-family detached lots less than 5,000-square feet and 50 percent of all single-family detached lots less than 8,000-square feet shall abut some form of open space.

Each Planning Area reflects the context in which it resides and each is planned in accordance with naturally occurring and existing infrastructure conditions. Flat lands characterize the Big Gulch Planning Area, and as a result, the majority of the community's density occurs there. This area may be characterized by the incorporation of many Smart Growth features, with buildings close to the main arterial roadways, pedestrian-friendly sidewalks, street trees and benches, shared surface parking and garages encouraged at the side, rear or within building clusters to reduce the amount of paving and empty space that define traditional parking lots. Housing would include apartments, townhouses, condominiums, patio homes and high-density, single-family detached and attached homes. The Highway Mixed-Use/Business Park area is connected to State Highway 16 and is designed to capitalize on that adjacency through a mixture of commercial, retail and business parks. As with Big Gulch, this area will include high-density single- and multi-family homes along with hotels.

Hills dominate the Northern Residential Planning Area and development will thin out as it moves northward. This area will be populated with a mix of low-density single- and multi-family homes. Two community parks and nine neighborhood parks are planned for this area, as well as sites for three elementary schools, two golf courses and a resort. The Southern Residential Planning Area contains the highest concentration of steep slopes, and in turn, units will be restricted to building envelopes that will reduce the visual impact of the development and maximize open space and trails. Development in the Southwestern Planning Area is anticipated to include rural and estate-type custom homes, with some of them part of an equestrian-themed neighborhood. An equestrian center, professionally operated and funded through the owner's association, will be a key feature of this neighborhood.

John Church, an economist and visiting professor at Boise State University, was hired by M3 to conduct a Demographic Forecast and Economic and Fiscal Impact Analysis of the proposed project as required by the city. Its primary objective was to estimate the fiscal impact that the M3 Eagle development would have upon affected public service providers, specifically Ada County, the City of Eagle, Meridian Joint School District No. 2, the Eagle Fire District, the Ada County Highway District, Ada County Emergency Medical Services, Ada County Weed and Pest Control and the Mosquito Abatement District. The analysis concluded that "the projected net fiscal impacts are universally positive." In the 20-year build out period, the projected total net fiscal impact to public service providers affected by the project would be:

The cost of fire and ambulance service was a point of dispute in Eagle's debate over annexation. Pictured: helicopter crew fights fire in the Boise Foothills, 2008.

U.S. Bureau of Land Management

- City of Eagle: +$23.20 million
- Ada County: +$81.98 million
- Ada County Highway District: +$64.91 million
- Ada County Emergency Medical Services: +$3.18 million
- Eagle Fire District: +$27.40 million
- Meridian Joint School District No. 2: +$116.18 million

Upon receipt of the report, the city hired Ben Johnson Associates, Inc. to conduct an independent review of the findings and report to the mayor and city council. Dr. Don Reading's analysis concluded that the Impact Analysis submitted by M3 Eagle was flawed in a number of areas. He disagreed on the net benefits and the projected costs, along with other calculations and assumptions. Conclusions about the project's viability and impact

concerned city leaders and highlighted issues raised by the foothills association and advocacy groups opposed to the development. The city sought clari-
fication on the discrepancies between the two reports. Church made an
appearance before the Eagle City Council and effectively rebutted Reading's
findings. Church explained in detail the methods and calculus underlying his
analysis and why it differed from the review. The council in turn accepted
the validity of the Church analysis in its further deliberations.

The city approved the Pre-Annexation and Development Agreement,
rezoning and project master plan in December of 2007 after Eagle amended
its comprehensive plan and gathered public and expert testimony. This culmi-
nated the process that began in 2006 with an initial application followed by
three heavily attended neighborhood meetings and 39 subsequent public
hearings and meetings with the city. While the final agreement may not
have included or addressed certain aspects that were highly prized by each
of the many stakeholders, it did significantly alter portions of the original
development plan, and the long and sustained process brought forth the
necessary changes that earned unanimous support from the Eagle City
Council.

Eagle annexed the M3 development on November 10, 2009. This land-
mark event allowed the developer to proceed with master traffic studies,
additional annexations into municipal districts and numerous other planning
processes that would bind it to the city and its infrastructure. Eagle roughly
doubled in size upon annexation, with a master plan calling for three elementary schools, a middle school and high school, public library, two fire stations and a police station all to be built on land donated by M3. The time-
frame for the full rollout of the community ranges between 20-35 years,
with capital infrastructure development accompanying community demand.
Annexation provides Eagle additional property tax revenues, however the
extent of their impact remains contingent upon growth and economic development.

As the process unfolds, additional obstacles remain and will challenge
long-standing stakeholder assumptions on numerous complex issues—two of
the most significant and far-reaching being water and land use. The developer became embroiled in a dispute with the Idaho Department of Water
Resources over their request for a water right, with the department ruling
against the initial request in December 2009. M3 had requested that it be
allowed to tap 23.18 cubic feet of water per second to supply the 17,000
residents who could one day reside in the 7,153 planned residences, secur-
ing an initial water right for the entirety of the development. The agency

denied this request and M3's subsequent request for reconsideration, and granted a lesser water right for the initial planning area with subsequent rights reviewed and granted as the development and roll out of planning areas proceeded. On January 25, 2010, Interim Director Gary Spackman produced an amended final order giving M3 approval for a water right with total flow rate diverted under the right not to exceed 3.28cfs. along with the total annual volume diverted to not exceed 923 acre-feet. M3 countered in the February 23, 2010 *Idaho Statesman*: "The hearing officer made an error, despite the overwhelming evidence provided that there is adequate storage of water in the underlying aquifer." An agreement signed on January 19, 2011 between M3 and the Idaho Department of Water Resources has opened the door for the City of Eagle to obtain a Reasonable Anticipation Future Needs Permit, a 30-year authorization that can only be issued to a municipality. M3 and Water Resources would have 60 days to work out the details under which the permit would be issued. If an arrangement is not reached, Jeff Peppersack, head of the department's water allocation bureau said the agreement "could still fall apart." Upon transference of M3's water permit to the city, the two sides would ask the Idaho District Court to dismiss M3's February 2010 lawsuit appealing Water Resource's rejection of the original water rights request and send the case back to Water Resources for a new decision.

Along with the water right dispute there remains continued debate over proposed land swaps between the BLM and M3. M3 owns a number of parcels of land in Idaho that could be traded for BLM landholdings in any number of configurations deemed beneficial to the company and BLM. These swaps have the potential to affect public use patterns and re-shuffle the groups that would most benefit from them. Any proposed swap of BLM lands around Eagle would rely on the completion of environmental impact studies and adherence to the "no net loss" provision within the development agreement with Eagle. In January of 2011, M3 revealed the foothills development previously referred to as M3 Eagle would be called Spring Valley in recognition of the McLeod family ranch from which most of the land was purchased. M3 is currently working on detailed planning for the infrastructure required for this first phase of the development, which is projected to begin late 2012 or early 2013, contingent upon market conditions.

The M3 Eagle development is just one example of the complex challenges surrounding growth and development that face Idaho communities. At this time, the process is still unfolding as issues of water rights, BLM land, endangered species and many other questions remain. The sheer number of interests and parties involved complicates matters but cannot be discounted or taken for granted. Changes in the political sphere may also affect the decision-making process and rearrange preferences. In October of 2010 Eagle swore in a new mayor, and it remains to be seen what change this will bring to public policy and the city's relation with the M3 development. While the M3 project has gathered support through the years, there still remains a vocal opposition to the development and some assumptions remain contested. Although city leaders and their publics may hold clear visions of the shape and nature they desire their communities to possess in the future, reconciling the demands of growth and its inherent private and public interests will remain a challenge.

• • •

Roman Lewis graduated in 2010 with a master's of public administration degree. He previously obtained a BS in political science from Boise State University. While studying for his MPA, he worked as a research assistant focusing on democratic institutions and collaborative governance.

Sources
•••••••••

Introduction

Ada County, Development Services, Ada County Comprehensive Plan, November 2007.

Ada County Open Space Advisory Task Force, Findings and Recommendations, April 22, 2008.

Anderson, Shea. "Sprawl: Its Making Us Fat: New Report Slams Idaho's Obesity Rates," *The Boise Weekly*, June 28, 2006.

City of Boise, Planning and Development Services, Boise City Comprehensive Plan, Goals, Objective and Policies, January 1997; updated with amendment, September 29, 2008.

"Our View: Valley residents pay energy price for suburban sprawl," *Idaho Statesman*, March 4, 2006.

William Yardley, "Boise Region Grapples With Smog," *New York Times*, January 22, 2009.

Ch 1: Managing Sprawl

American Farmland Trust. "Farmland Protection." American Farmland Trust website, undated.

Arnold, Joseph. *The New Deal in the Suburbs: A History of the Greenbelt Town Program*, 1935-1954. Columbus: Ohio State University Press, 1971.

Blake, Peter. *God's Own Junkyard: The Planned Deterioration of America's Landscape*. New York: Holt, Rinehart and Winston, 1964.

Burton, Hal. "Trouble in the Suburbs." *The Saturday Evening Post*, September 17, 1955.

City of Boise. *Blueprint Boise*. Boise: City of Boise, 2010.

Gillham, Oliver. *The Limitless City: A Primer on the Urban Sprawl Debate*. Washington, D.C.: Island Press, 2002.

Harrison, Rick. *Prefurbia: Reinventing the Suburbs: From Disdainable to Sustainable*. Dubuque: Sustainable Land Development International, 2008.

Hoyt, Homer. *The Structure and Growth of Residential Neighborhoods in American Cities*. Washington, D.C.: Federal Housing Administration, 1939.

Hurd, Richard. *Principles of City Land Values*. New York: The Record and Guide, 1903.

Jacobs, Jane. *The Death and Life of Great American Cities*. New York: Vintage Books, 1961.

Katz, Peter. *The New Urbanism: Toward an Architecture of Community*. New York: McGraw-Hill Professional, 1993.

Meter, Ken. "Greater Treasure Valley Region (Southwest Idaho & Eastern Oregon) Local Farm & Food Economy." Idaho Smart Growth website, June 2010.

Mumford, Lewis. *The City in History: Its Origins, Its Transformations, and Its Prospects*. New York: Harcourt Brace Jovanovich, Inc., 1961.

Mumford, Lewis. *The Highway and the City*. New York: Harcourt, Brace, & World, Inc., 1963.

Peterson, Jon. *The Birth of City Planning in the United States, 1840-1917*. Baltimore: The Johns Hopkins University Press, 2003.

Reilly, William. ed. *The Use of Land: A Citizens' Policy Guide to Urban Growth*. New York: Thomas Y. Crowell Company, 1973.

Soule, David, ed. *Urban Sprawl: A Comprehensive Reference Guide*. Westport: Greenwood Press, 2006.

Thompson, Edward, Jr. "'Hybrid' Farmland Protection Programs: A New Paradigm for Growth Management?" *William and Mary Environmental Law and Policy Review*, 1999.

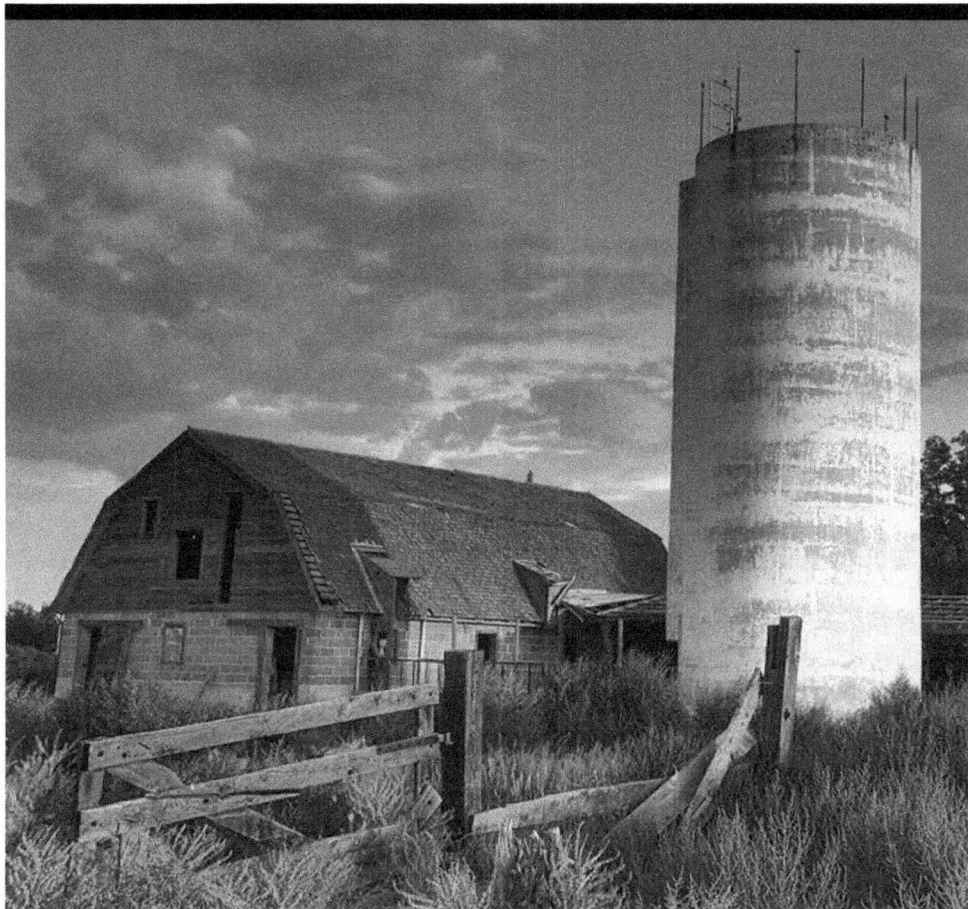

Charles Knowles

Sprawl critics look to conservation easements to slow the spread of housing that consumes agricultural lands. Pictured: vanishing farmland near Star.

Urban Land Institute. *High Density Development: Myth and Fact*. Washington, D.C.: Urban Land Institute, 2005.

Weber, Adna Ferrin. *The Growth of Cities in the Nineteenth Century: A Study in Statistics*. Ithaca: Cornell University Press, 1899.

U.S. Environmental Protection Agency, U.S. Department of Transportation, and U.S. Department of Housing and Urban Development. "HUD-DOT-EPA Partnership for Sustainable Communities." EPA website, October 21. 2010.

Ch. 2: Streetcar Suburbs

"Activity In The West End." *Idaho Daily Statesman*, May 23, 1905.

Ada County Assessor's Office. *Fairview Addition to Boise City, Idaho*. Boise: Ada County, 1903.

Ada County Assessor's Office. *Hubbell Home Addition to Boise City, Idaho*. Boise: Ada County, 1910.

Ada County Assessor's Office. *Plat of Frank Davis Addition to Boise City*, Idaho. Boise: Ada County, 1910.

Ada County Assessor's Office. *Plat of Pleasanton Addition to Boise City, Idaho*. Boise: Ada County, 1908.

Ada County Assessor's Office. *Plat of West Side Addition to Boise*. Boise: Ada County, 1905.

"A Long Pursed Man." *Idaho Daily Statesman*, November 15, 1903.

"Big Majority Is for Entrance to City." *Idaho Daily Statesman*, March 10, 1912.

Casner, Nick and Valeri Kiesig. *Trolley: Boise Valley's Electric Road 1891-1928*. Boise: Black Canyon Communications, 2002.

"City's Buildings Attest Its Advance." *Idaho Daily Statesman*, October 11, 1909, Boise.

Idaho's Highway History 1863-1975. Boise: Idaho Transportation Department, 1985.

Insurance Maps, Boise, Idaho. New York: Sanborn Map Company, 1912.

Insurance Maps, Boise, Idaho. New York: Sanborn Map Company, 1949.

"Involves Title to Fair Grounds." *Idaho Daily Statesman*, April 9, 1904.

Keyser Marston Associates Inc. 30th Street Urban Renewal Area Eligibility Report Prepared for the Capital City Development Corporation. Boise: Capital City Development Corporation, September 1, 2008.

"Legal Notices." *Idaho Daily Statesman*, December 3, 1912.

MacGregor, Carol Lynn. Boise, Idaho 1882-1910: *Prosperity in Isolation*. Missoula, MT: Mountain Press, 2006.

Neil, J. Meredith. "City Limits: The Emergence of Metropolitan Boise 1945-2006." Unpublished draft, 2006.

Planning and Development Services, City of Boise. "Parcel Level Analysis: Residential and Commercial Structure Built," Boise: City of Boise, 2007.

"Planing Mill Running." *Idaho Daily Statesman*, January 20, 1906.

"Pleasanton Residents Out." *Idaho Daily Statesman*, July 23, 1911.

Pomeroy, Earl. *The Pacific Slope: A History of California, Oregon, Washington, Idaho, Utah, and Nevada*. New York: Alfred A. Knopf, 1965.

"Proclamation." *Idaho Daily Statesman*, November 29, 1903.

Reps, John W. *Cities of the American West: A History of Frontier Urban Planning*. Princeton: Princeton University Press, 1979.

Shallat, Todd, ed. *Harrison Boulevard: Preserving the Past in Boise's North End*. Boise: Boise State University School of Social Sciences and Public Affairs, 1989.

Stacy, Susan. Tom and Julia Davis: "Some Good Place," Boise, Idaho. Boise: T & J Publishers, 2007.

TAG Historical Research and Consulting. "Survey Report: Sand Creek Proposed Cell Tower." Boise: TAG Historical Research Consulting, April, 2007.

"The West Side Addition." *Idaho Daily Statesman*, April 23, 1905.

"Three Additions May Come to Town Today." *Idaho Daily Statesman*, March 9, 1912.

"Three Additions Now A Part Of Boise City." *Idaho Daily Statesman*, March 14, 1912.

"Two Additions Want To Be In City." *Idaho Daily Statesman*, February 7, 1912.

Warner, Jr., Sam Bass. *Streetcar Suburbs: The Process of Growth in Boston 1870-1900*. Cambridge: Harvard University Press, 1962.

Wells, Merle and Arthur Hart. *Boise: An Illustrated History*. Sun Valley: American Historical Press, 2000.

Ch. 3: Catching Up with Kuna

Behunin, Troy. Interview, October 7, 2010.

Brunt, Jonathan. "Kuna Battles Growth to Maintain its Identity." *Idaho Statesman*, April 28, 2003.

City of Kuna. "Kuna 2009 Comprehensive Plan." City of Kuna website, undated.

"Conservation." Western Heritage Historic Byway website, undated

Dowdy, Scott. Interview, October 7, 2010.

Estrella, Joe. "Group: Smart Growth? Not in Kuna." *Idaho Statesman*, March 13, 2004.

Franden, John. Interview, January 12, 2011.

Hasson, Steve. Interview, October 7, 2010.

Hubbard, D.R. "Kuna." Idaho State Historical Library and Archives, Boise, 1909

Hummel, Jay. Interview, January 12, 2011.

Kreller, Kathleen. "Kuna Funds Police, Sewers, Planning." *Idaho Statesman*, August 27, 2004.

Kreller, Kathleen. "Kuna Growth Again Nearly Surpasses Sewer Limits." *Idaho Statesman*, February 28, 2005.

"Kuna." *Idaho Tri-Weekly Statesman*, September 6, 1883.

"Kuna Growing Too Fast." Meridian: *Valley News*, 1979.

Lamanna, John. Interview, October 7, 2010.

Peregrine Fund. "World Center for Birds of Prey." World Center for Birds of Prey website, undated.

Talbutt, Brad. "Developers Look to Annex 3,400 acres into Kuna." *Idaho Statesman*, January 28, 2008.

Smart Growth. "Principles of Smart Growth." Smart Growth website, undated.

Tucker, John. "Kuna is Turning into Next Meridian." *Idaho Statesman*, February 9, 1999.

Walgamott, Charles. Six Decades Back (*Idaho Yesterdays*). Moscow: University of Idaho Press, 1990.

Ch. 4: Hidden Springs

Allen, Gary. Interview, October 17, 2010.

Congress for the New Urbanism. "Charter of the New Urbanism." Congress for the New Urbanism website, 1996.

Etlinger, Charles. "New frontier opens at Hidden Springs." *Idaho Statesman*, April 17, 1999.

Farnsworth, Christina. "Urban Range." Builder 24, No. 3, 2001.

Hidden Springs website, undated.

Hoffman, Nathaniel. "No Work Here." *Boise Weekly*, January 7, 2009.

Horan, Tiffany. "Hidden Springs- Neighbors Build a Community." *Idaho Statesman*, January 16, 2000.

Hummel, Charles. Interview, October 16, 2010.

Idaho Smart Growth. "Smart Growth Best Practices-Putting Smart Growth Policy into Practice." Idaho Smart Growth website, undated.

Kolman, Joe. "Some Hidden Springs Residents Upset Over Plans for 102 New Homes." *Idaho Statesman*, July 28, 2003.

Quintana, Craig. "Hidden Springs Homes Cluster on Flat Land, Leaving Hillsides Open." *Idaho Statesman*, April 10, 2000.

Sewell, Cynthia. "Boise Takes Ada County to Court Over Planned Community." *Idaho Statesman*, March 9, 2006.

Simnitt, Emily. "Hidden Springs is Finalist for Award." *Idaho Statesman*, January 11, 2001.

Waag, William. Interview, June 27, 2010.

Wyatt, Liz. "Hidden Springs Development to Build its own Police, Fire Station." *Idaho Statesman*, July 22, 1999.

Ch. 5: Bown Crossing

Alder, Jerry. "Bye, Bye Suburban Dream." *Newsweek* , May 15, 1995.

Boise City Council and the Planning and Zoning Commission. Subdivision Design Work Session. Boise: City of Boise, 2004.

Catt, Aaron. "Construction Begins in Bown Crossing." Boise Real Estate Soup, January 28, 2010.

City of Boise. Boise City Planning and Zoning Commission Minutes. March 1, 2004.

City of Boise. Boise's Zoning Code. City of Boise website, undated.

City of Boise. "Commercial Infill Projects-Bown Crossing." City of Boise website. Undated.

Congress for the New Urbanism. "Network Preamble: CNU Statements of Principles on Transportation Networks." Congress for the New Urbansim website, undated.

Congress for the New Urbanism. "Walkable Thoroughfares Guide." Congress for the New Urbanism website, undated.

Dekerchove, N. Interview, June 29, 2010.

Dryden, C. "Music, Children's Activities Part of the Fun at Bown Crossing's Monthly Parties." Knight Ridder Tribune Business News, August 10, 2007.

Duany, Andres, Elizabeth Plater-Zyberk and Jeff Speck. *Suburban Nation: The Rise of Sprawl and the Decline of the American Dream*. New York: North Point Press, 2001.

Florida, Richard. *The Rise of the Creative Class: And How It's Transforming Work, Leisure, Community and Everyday Life*. New York: Basic Books, 2002.

Hayman, Nick and Aaron Mondada. "The Bown House." Boise Architecture Project website, 2009.

Jacobs, Allan. Great Streets. Cambridge: The MIT Press, 1995.

Linenberger, R. Interview, October 20, 2010.

McKibben, Sherry. "Planet: The Power of Place." Lunch and Lead: Sustainable Business Practices, Boise, Idaho, December 2, 2010.

Moeller, Katy. "New Subdivisions Will Bring Urban Feel to Eagle: Four Planned High-Density Developments." *Idaho Statesman*, April 16, 2007.

O'Neill, Derick. Interview, June 30, 2010.

O'Neill Enterprises. "Creating Communities of Exceptional and Lasting Value." O'Neill Enterprises website, undated.

O'Neill, Peter. Interview, October 27, 2010.

Simmons, Hal. Interview, October 27, 2010.

Stewart, Bethann. "For the Business Owners in Boise's Bown Crossing, New Bridge Is Just the Beginning." *Idaho Statesman*, May 13, 2010.

Title One. "Title One CCRs and Plat Map." Title One, A Title and Escrow Company website, undated.

Urban Land Institute. "Land Use and Driving: The Role Compact Development Can Play in Reducing Greenhouse Gas Emissions." Urban Land Institute website. Undated.

Webb, Anna. "If They Still Make It, We've Got It." Knight Ridder Tribune Business News, January 14, 2007.

High-density infill has contributed to the revitalization of Boise's urban core. Pictured: crowding into The Balcony at 8th and Idaho.

Stonethorn/Flickr

Ch. 6: Once There Were Trees

Agricultural Air Quality Task Force. "Air Quality Policy on Agricultural Burning." U.S. Department of Agriculture Natural Resources Conservation Service website, 2000.

BLM Four River Field Office and Gem County. "Community Economic Profile—Gem County." Gem County website, undated.

City of Emmett. "City of Emmett Fiscal Impact Report, July 5, 2005." City of Emmett website, undated.

Ch. 7: Does Dense Make Sense?

Bieter, David. "State of the City 2005: Boise, A Neighborhood City by Design." City of Boise website, September 15, 2005.

Boise City Clerk. "City Council Meeting Minutes, August 31, 2005." City of Boise website.

Boise City Clerk. "City Council Meeting Minutes, September 1, 2005." City of Boise website.

Boise City Planning & Development Services. "Boise City Disinvestment Monitoring Report, April 12, 2000." City of Boise website.

Boise City Planning & Development Services. "Boise City Planning & Zoning Commission Hearing Minutes of January 10, 2005." City of Boise website.

Boise City Planning & Development Services. "Boise City Planning & Zoning Commission Hearing Minutes of May 4, 2005." City of Boise website.

Boise City Planning & Development Services. "Planning Division Staff Report CUP05-00015, May 4, 2005." City of Boise website.

Boise City Planning & Development Services. "Planning Division Staff Report CUP04-00117, December 13, 2004." City of Boise website.

City of Boise. Blueprint Boise. Boise: City of Boise, 2010.

Clark Development. "Introduction." Clark Development website, undated.

Clark, Bill. "Crescent Rim development meets criteria of community." *Idaho Statesman*, October 23. 2004.

Clark, Bill. Interview, September 24, 2010.

Clark, Bill. Interview, January 11, 2011.

Clegg, Elaine. Interview, January 7, 2011.

"Crescent Rim Development Meets Criteria of Community." *Idaho Statesman*, October 23, 2004.

Depot Bench Neighborhood Association. "Depot Bench Neighborhood Plan." DBNA website, October 2007.

Idaho Smart Growth and Urban Land Institute. "Quality Infill Recommendations and Tools." Idaho Smart Growth website, undated.

"Letters to the Editor: Crescent Rim." *Idaho Statesman*, September 14, 2005.

Oshohi, Denise. "Crescent Rim Condo Hearing Draws Crowd to P&Z Meeting." *Idaho Statesman*, May 5, 2005.

Oshodi, Denise. "Neighbors Take Initiative to Promote Quality Infill." *Idaho Statesman*, July 18.

Thompson, Russ. Interview, September 29, 2010.

Wolf, Carrisa. "Size Matters on the Boise Bench." *Boise Weekly*, December 29, 2004.

Ch. 8: Moving Target

Barker, Rocky. "Can We Head off Ozone Crackdown?" *Idaho Statesman*, March 20, 2008.

Barker, Rocky. "The Valley Crosses Line on Ozone." *Idaho Statesman*, July 30, 2008.

Buckendorf, Madeline and Chuck Randolph. "Looping the Loop." *Idaho Press Tribune*, July 30, 2007.

COMPASS. "Products and Services—Communities in Motion 2035 UPDATE." Community Planning Association of Southwest Idaho website, undated.

COMPASS. "Products and Services—Multimodal Center." Community Planning Association of Southwest Idaho website, undated.

COMPASS. "Products & Services—Treasure Valley High Capacity Transit Study." Community Planning Association of Southwest Idaho website, undated.

Congress for the New Urbanism. "Who Is CNU?" Congress for the New Urbanism website, undated.

Davis, L. J. "Tearing Down Boise." *Harper's*, November 1974.

Hovee & Company. "Portland Streetcar Development Impacts. Portland, OR, Capital City Development Corp." Capital Development Corporation Boise website, undated.

Jalbert, Rhonda. Interview, January 13, 2011.

Sewell, Cynthia. "Time for New Levy?—Many Boiseans Are Ready, Again, to Pay for Foothills Open Space." *Idaho Statesman*, March 28, 2010.

Sewell, Cynthia. "Transit Center Plan Still Stirring Debate—One of Downtown Boise's Biggest Developers Warns Against the 11th Street Site." *Idaho Statesman*, May 6, 2010.

Sobel, Lee, Steven Bodzin, Ellen Greenberg, Jonathan Miller, and John Norquist. *Greyfields Into Goldfields: Dead Malls Become Living Neighborhoods*. Chicago: Congress for the New Urbanism, 2002.

Webb, Anna. "Take a walk into the past." *Idaho Statesman*, June 24, 2006.

Whyte, William. *Social Life of Small Urban Places*. Ann Arbor: Project for Public Spaces, 1980.

U.S. Census Bureau. *1970 Census of Population and Housing: Final Population Counts* Washington, DC: U.S. Government Printing Office, 2000.

Ch. 9: Biking Boise

Ada County Consortium. "Blueprint for Good Growth." Blueprint for Good Growth website, undated.

Ada County Highway District. "Roadways to Bikeways Plan." Ada County Highway District, 2009.

Bernard, Josh. "Electric City: Transforming the Boise Valley." Boise City Office of the Historian website, undated.

Casner, Nick and Valeri Kiesig. *Trolly: Boise Valley's Electric Road 1891-1928*. Boise: Black Canyon Communications, LLC., 2002.

Fackelmann, Kathleen. "Studies Tie Urban Sprawl to Health Risks, Road Danger." *USA Today*, August 28, 2003.

Franden, John. Interview, January 12, 2011.

Wray, J. Harry. Pedal Power: *The Quiet Rise of the Bicycle in American Public Life*. Boulder: Paradigm Publishers, 2008.

Ch. 10: Beyond Eagle

Bandy, Phil. 2009 Property Tax Levy Rate. City of Eagle website, undated.

Bandy, Phil. Interview, October 14, 2010.

Ben Johnson Associates, Inc. A Review of M3-Eagle Development Demographic Forecast Economic & Fiscal Impact Analysis. Boise: Ben Johnson Associates, Inc., 2007.

Church, Dr. John. M3 Economic Report- Economic Impact Analysis & Demographic Forecast. Idaho Department of Water Resources website, undated.

City of Eagle. "Pre-Annexation and Development Agreement by and between City of Eagle and M3 Eagle L.L.C." Eagle: City of Eagle, 2007.

Estrella, Joe. "It's Official: M3's Eagle Foothills Development Will be Called Spring Valley." *Idaho Statesman*, January 3, 2011.

Estrella, Joe. "M3 Eagle Takes Water Fight to Court." *Idaho Statesman*, February 23, 2010.

Idaho Department of Water Resources. "Application to Appropriate Water No. 63-32573 In The Name of M3 Eagle LLC.AMENDED FINAL ORDER." IDWR website, undated.

North Ada County Foothills Association. "An Introduction to NACFA." North Ada County Foothills Association website, undated.

Robbins, Gerry. Interview, October 4, 2010.

Scott Peyron & Associates. "M3 Eagle Engages Idaho's Universities to Conduct Multi-Year Studies in North Ada County and Eagle Foothills." August 30, 2006.

Sewell, Cynthia. "Development Would Double Size of Eagle." *Idaho Statesman*, October 13, 2006.

U.S. Census Bureau. Estimated Population By State: 2000-2009. Washington, D.C.: U.S. Government Printing Office, 2009.

U.S. Census Bureau. Population Estimates Branch, Estimated Population by State: 2000-2009. Washington, D.C.: U.S. Government Printing Office, 2009.

U.S. Census Bureau. Table 4: Annual Estimates of the Resident Population for Incorporated Places in Idaho: April 1, 2000 to July 1, 2009. Washington, D.C.: U.S. Government Printing Office, 2009.

Boise State University

Boise State University, with an enrollment of more than 19,000 students, is a progressive student-focused university dedicated to excellence in teaching, innovative research, leadership development and community service. Its students benefit from an emphasis on the undergraduate experience, including public affairs research as demonstrated by the student papers in this publication.

With record student enrollment, new academic buildings, additional degree programs and an expanding research portfolio, it is no coincidence that in 2009 Boise State was ranked by *U.S. News & World Report* among the nation's "top up-and-coming schools." With Idaho's fastest-growing research program, Boise State is in the midst of a transformation that builds on its traditional teaching strengths while expanding its capabilities in research and scholarly activity. This evolution reflects the integral role that Boise State plays in contributing to the quality of life in the Treasure Valley and beyond.

www.ingramcontent.com/pod-product-compliance
Lightning Source LLC
Chambersburg PA
CBHW072138020426
42334CB00018B/1850